SUICIDE RISK

Not that suicide always comes from madness. There are said to be occasions when a wise man takes that course: but, generally speaking, it is not in an access of reasonableness that people kill themselves.

—Voltaire

The more mature a relationship, the more able the two people are to give up their dependency and learn how to live alone together.

—Elvin Semrad

SUICIDE RISK

The Formulation of Clinical Judgment

John T. Maltsberger, M. D.

NEW YORK UNIVERSITY PRESS
New York & London

Details of the cases discussed in this book, with the exception of those explicitly attributed to other sources, are well known to the author. In each instance, however, the identity of all individuals has been carefully disguised in order to make them unrecognizable to the public.

Library of Congress Cataloging-in-Publication Data

Maltsberger, John T.
Suicide risk.

Bibliography: p. 161.
Includes index.
1. Suicide. 2. Health risk assessment. I. Title.
RC569.M35 1986   616.85'844505   86-2415
ISBN 0-8147-5398-1 (alk. paper)

Clothbound editions of New York University Press Books are Smyth-sewn and printed on permanent and durable acid-free paper.

Book design by Ken Venezio

c 10 9 8 7 6 5 4 3 2

In grateful memory of
Elvin V. Semrad
and to
Dan H. Buie, Jr.

Contents

Introduction

No challenge in clinical psychiatry can be more stressful or demanding than understanding, correctly appraising, and managing the patient who threatens suicide. At the beginning of psychiatric training the task seems almost insuperable; students must have careful teaching and emotional support to master the challenge. The burden is equally heavy for trainees in other disciplines who shoulder responsibility for the daily care of suicidal patients.

More than twenty years ago Dan H. Buie and I, finishing our formal psychiatric training and smarting from first experiences with suicide, began to study these patients. Our collaboration has continued to the present. Initially we studied a group of suicides at the Massachusetts Mental Health Center in Boston, greatly assisted by the collaborative, cooperative spirit of our colleagues and the hospital staff.

After we published a paper or two others learned of our interest in the problem. We were invited by other colleagues to review suicides and serious suicide attempts at other psychiatric centers in and around Boston. More recently we have been invited to discuss similar experiences with colleagues in other cities of the United States and Canada who wanted to learn how we understood suicidal problems.

Our clinical study led us to an understanding that helps assess the danger of suicide, decide whether or not hospitalization is indicated, plan treatment, determine the readiness for hospital discharge, and guide psychotherapy. The psychiatric community here has found it useful, and in some ways it is unique, although it arises from long established principles of psychoanalytic psychiatry. We call it psychodynamic formulation.

Our slowness to publish a description of the formulation of suicide risk arose from a mutual perception that we had not, after all, come on anything particularly new. Elvin Semrad, our teacher, consistently emphasized the importance of formulating each new case as he guided our training in history taking and mental status examination. He regularly referred to the formulative work of his teacher, J. C. Whitehorn, and repeatedly encouraged his residents to read the article Whitehorn had written about it. So strongly did he feel about this article that he had it reprinted and gave every new resident a copy (Whitehorn 1944). All of us knew that Whitehorn was "formulating" cases years ago.

That we applied the principles of case formulation to a series of suicide cases was therefore natural enough; our perspective on suicide did not appear particularly unusual to us or to the men and women who shared our training. Only later did we gather that the teachings of Whitehorn and Semrad were not universally appreciated throughout our profession. Indeed, when we began to look, we discovered that their formulative approach, though often implied, was not explicitly elaborated in the suicide literature. Discussions with many colleagues have satisfied us that the formulative perspective is unfamiliar to many.

After our work had been presented at a number of conferences many colleagues began to ask for a written description of psychodynamic formulation in suicide. We prepared an article which proved too long for one of the major journals; rather than abridge it, we published it privately. Appearing in 1983, it was entitled "The Practical Formulation of Suicide Risk." Though we distributed it as widely as we could, and many who heard of it by word of mouth were kind enough to send for a copy, we were not publishing professionals. It was never widely circulated and remained mostly unknown, although a second printing was necessary. The pamphlet was really too brief to give the fullest treatment to the subject, in any case.

In 1984 we were approached by the New York University Press with the suggestion that an expanded version of that pamphlet ought to be made available to a wider professional audience. We eagerly agreed, and the result you have before you.

Whitehorn sowed the seeds of the formulative approach; Semrad tended and propagated the vines; we have pressed some of the grapes and can claim only a portion of credit if the wine is good. So it is with this book. The seminal ideas here, to the extent they belong to either of us, are Buie's as much as they are mine. We have turned them over many times together in discussing many suicidal cases. That I appear as sole author is very likely misleading.

As Dr. Buie was much engaged with other work we agreed that I would assume responsibility for expanding our original pamphlet into a larger manuscript. Hoping to achieve greater clarity, I have introduced a number of case illustrations. I have discussed most of our ideas much.more fully; our original pamphlet was in fact almost telegraphic in its brief twenty-two pages.

The work of other authors has received more attention here. Other approaches to estimating suicide risk receive at least a cursory notice. These can alert the examiner to the possibility of suicide danger as he begins to study a new patient. I have added a good deal of new material concerning the developmental difficulties that dispose to suicidal danger.

This book has been written with particular concern for younger colleagues beginning their professional training. They need every help they can obtain. The distress suicidal patients can provoke in those who must take responsibility for dealing with them (especially late at night in busy emergency rooms) is formidable. If what is written here eases their way I shall be well rewarded.

Enough history and patient observation can be obtained in about an hour to make an intelligent case formulation. A little practice improves efficiency, a fact which I hope readers unfamiliar with the formulative approach will demonstrate for themselves. An occasional patient may take longer; many of the more puzzling cases will obviously require admission to the hospital where there will be a more extended opportunity for interviewing.

Dr. Buie has combed the text, enabling me to remove mistakes and to correct several omissions. Thanks are due Dr. Laurence Chud, whose careful reading also resulted in a number of improvements. Permission to reprint the "suicide risk estimator" included in the appendix has been graciously extended by Publications Services Division of the American Psychiatric Association, which holds the copyright, and by its senior author, Dr. Jerome Motto.

JOHN T. MALTSBERGER

Boston, Massachusetts
January 1986

SUICIDE RISK

1.

Vulnerability to Suicide

To understand the vulnerability to suicide is to understand the psychology of despair. Experienced clinicians sense that depression, psychosis, or other mental suffering is taking on a new and darker color when they ask a patient, "Have you given up on yourself?"

Giving up on Oneself

Profound depression may invite suicide, but many patients in such a state maintain enough hope to live through their suffering, trusting in an eventual recovery. When such a patient despairs, however, the danger grows. The lowering of spirits and dejected attitude of melancholy are not incompatible with hope for future improvement. But some depressed patients despair. They feel powerless, surrender hope, give up on themselves. They are sure there will be no getting better. Clinical studies have demonstrated that despair is more highly correlated with suicide (and serious attempts) than depression is, and we know, further, that schizophrenic patients are particularly likely to destroy themselves when they surrender hope of recovering (Beck 1975; Wetzel 1976; Minkoff 1973; Drake 1984; Yarden 1982).

People vary greatly in their capacity to maintain hope. Some are easily discouraged; the optimist who looks cheerfully to the future whatever blows he may suffer may seem little more than a fool to the pessimist, ready to give up when life gives him a little knock. Some people give way to suicide when in reality much remains to them of an encouraging nature. Others, such as the survivors of Nazi concentration camps, where comparatively few suicides took place, demonstrate courage of heroic dimensions in horrible circumstances.

Neurochemical research has now disclosed certain substances in the cerebrospinal fluid of despairing patients who stand on the verge of suicide. These compounds do not occur in comparable amounts in that of deeply depressed patients who are not suicidal (Asberg 1976; Traskman 1981). The meaning of this finding from the developmental point of view is not clear; it may well be that the disposition to despair and the appearance of such a metabolite (5-hydroxyindole acetic acid for example) in the spinal fluid are both the consequence of a common genetic misfortune that renders the patient incapable of hope under stress. As yet there is no evidence for this view; it is not unreasonable to speculate that persons who suffer emotional injuries in childhood not only may later prove vulnerable to despair, but, as a consequence of early traumatization, may when despairing secrete such substances. At present we do not know whether the coincidence of these spinal fluid metabolites and states of despair reflects the operation of inheritance or trauma; possibly both are involved.

Let us set aside the biological aspects of despair for the moment; as yet, they are little understood. It will be clinically more useful to review some theoretical points that bear on the psychology of despair, namely, anxiety mastery and self-esteem regulation.

The subjective experience of despair has two parts. First, the patient finds himself in an intolerable affective state, flooded with emotional pain so intense and so unrelenting that it can no longer be endured. Second, the patient recognizes his condition, and gives up on himself. This recognition is not merely a cognitive surrender, even though most hopeless patients probably have thought about their circumstances and reach conscious, cognitive conclusions to give up. A more important aspect of the recognition I am describing is an unconscious, precognitive operation in which the self is abandoned as being unworthy of further concern.

First of all let me address three affect states that may rapidly become unendurable; often they force patients to commit suicide. These are *aloneness, self-contempt*, and *murderous rage*. I shall have something to say about each of these in turn, beginning the discussion of aloneness by inviting the reader's attention to how children learn to master early experiences of terror.

In the course of development as the child matures toward adulthood a series of danger situations must be successfully mastered for future psychic health. Initially the small infant grows alarmed if it senses that it is in physical danger (from cold, thirst, or hunger, for instance), quickly associating the experience of relief with the helping responses of its mother. As the mother is recognized as a separate person, the child begins to experience separation anxiety, sensing that separation from her renders him vulnerable. Later, as the child recognizes himself as a separate discrete, and non-omnipotent individual with his own body, valuing it and its pleasure-giving functions, fears of mutilation and loss of precious parts of himself arise— he learns that painful injury and loss are possible. This is called castration anxiety; it denotes not only fear of genital loss or damage, but the fear of loss or mutilation of other parts of the body as well. As development proceeds, the child learns to fear not only the loss of his mother's presence as a comforter and protector, but to fear the loss of her love, and the loss of its father's love also, without which he cannot sustain a sense of self-worth. Finally, as the values and approval-giving functions of the parents are internalized and become a part of the developing child himself, there is the danger, this time an inner one, of losing the approval of the superego, the inner heir of the parents; healthy adults need to give themselves a vote of confidence.

In discussing these various danger situations Freud (1926) spoke of the potential helplessness of the individual in each. The infant, unrelieved by its mother, will quickly move toward physiological disaster and the subjective experiences which accompany it if its needs go unmet. The child a little older, abandoned by his mother before he has the capacity to soothe his own distress when left alone, is vulnerable to emotional disaster. The child who cannot prevent himself from being physically injured, or who perceives himself in immediate danger of such injury that he cannot avoid, will be flooded with the affects of disaster. So with the child who believes he has lost his parents' love irremediably, and so with the adult who abandons himself as irremediably unlovable. Those children who are protected from the full development of separation terror because the adults about them are adequately and empathically responsive learn to respond optimistically when small amounts of separation anxiety are aroused. Soothed repeatedly over time in a consistent, capable way, the child builds up his hope-giving experiences into a kind of separation-optimism, becoming tolerant of separation for longer and longer periods of time, gradually learning to endure solitude without unreasonable distress.

The child who is not so fortunate, however, will be subject from time to time to overwhelming separation terror, and, failing to receive the hope-giving soothing of dependable, empathic adults, will experience distress of great intensity. This overwhelming distress, the agony of helplessness, Freud called *au-*

tomatic anxiety, and the situation giving rise to it, the *traumatic situation*. A child subjected to too many occasions of unmodulated, massive anxiety will not develop an optimistic attitude to occasions of emotional danger. When despair and dread (or their infantile affective prologues) color the days, weeks, and months as infancy and early childhood pass by, the maturing adult will lack the capacity to respond to distressing circumstances with the modulated suffering called *signal anxiety*. Signal anxiety implies hope for the future and invites appropriate adaptive, corrective behavior. Instead, he will react with intense, primitive, unmodulated anxiety; paralysis may ensue, no adaptive behavior is possible, and despair threatens unless someone intervenes from outside. Later writers have developed these ideas, elaborating the central theme that helplessness in the face of external danger, or helplessness in the face of intolerable affect, is not consistent with self-esteem and ultimately invites self-repudiation.

The extensive literature on early child development cannot be reviewed here, but Klein (1975) has discussed early fears of annihilation, and Mahler (1975) the vicissitudes of early separation experiences. Instead, I shall elaborate one psychoanalytic line, based on Freud's anxiety theory, which should suffice for present purposes.

Bibring (1953) described depression as an ego state whose main characteristics are "a decrease of self-esteem, a more or less intense state of helplessness, a more or less intensive and extensive inhibition of functions, and a more or less intensely felt particular emotion. . . ." He argued that it arose when the ego was unable to achieve some aspiration forcibly held out by the ego-ideal, commonly a demand to be worthy, loved, appreciated, to be competent and strong, or to be loving and good. He compared it with the feeling of anxiety and classed anxiety and depression together as basic ego reactions. "Anxiety as a reaction to (external or internal) danger indicates the ego's desire to survive. The ego, challenged by the danger, mobilizes the signal of anxiety and prepares for fight or flight."

Bibring was describing signal anxiety here, the anxiety of the healthy optimistic adult, in which the massive, primitive automatic anxiety of early traumatic situations has been transformed into an activating response, implying hope for more comfortable adaptation.

"In depression," he continued, "the opposite takes place, the ego is paralyzed because it finds itself incapable to meet the 'danger.' In extreme situations the wish to live is replaced by the wish to die." The patient who has some hope of successful adaptation in a danger situation is responding with signal anxiety; the patient who reacts with helplessness and surrenders hope responds with depression.

The question now arises, how does the child learn to master separation distress without immediate appeal to his mother's physical presence? It is a commonplace that such a development takes place, but what is involved? Before attempting to answer these questions I should like to spell out an assumption which will underlie the discussion to follow. It is this—that under the influence of the baby's relationship with his mother certain mental *structures* will develop that in time will replace what the mother does for him by way of emotional regulation. Structure as I shall use the term refers to a group of lasting capacities for self-regulation, organized from the melding together of emotional impulses and responses, and the reactions to these by others, that are taken into the mind of the developing person as a continuing part of himself. Although in discussing the development of regulatory structures we shall continue to concentrate on the mother-child relationship, it should be noted that factors other than the quality of the relationship the mother and child are able to create together will surely influence the extent to which effective, stable structures can be built. Among these are the quality and intensity of the child's emotional reactions themselves, physical illnesses, the child's innate capacity for structure development, and genetic influences.

The failure to internalize would appear to have some relationship to the complaint of feeling empty, so common among people who are suicide prone. If psychoanalysis has clarified anything about human nature, it must be that a person is incapable of feeling sufficient, competent, peaceful or reasonably worthwhile without experiencing a state of competence, peace, and love early in life built up in collaboration with his mother. She regulates tension and makes a sense of safety and comfort possible. Life may later prove unendurable unless through internalizing those regulatory functions a person develops the capacity to settle himself. Otherwise he must find someone else to regulate him from the outside as his mother once should have, or turn to drugs, psychosis, perversion, or suicide to secure some relief from mental pain. All the danger situations detailed by Freud have in common this theme—separation from a source of comfort external to the core of the self. That source may be a person or some structural derivation of a human relationship, e.g., a comforting introject, but a sense of psychic closeness to a comforting presence is essential throughout life if regression to a state of primary, automatic anxiety of agonizing proportions is to be avoided.

The overpowering affect of *aloneness* which makes life unendurable for a large number of suicidal individuals can be understood within the general class of primary (automatic) anxiety. The eerie devastation of adult aloneness (not loneliness) probably repeats the empty hours of an infancy where no empathic soothing was available to relieve imperative needs and fearful tensions.

Certain aspects of the aloneness experience would seem to tie it to such early traumatic situations. Aloneness as an affect certainly implies separation from any comfort-giving resource, but unlike the experience of ordinary and familiar loneliness, it contains no hopeful intimation that the state of being cut off from others will ever be relieved (Winnicott 1958; Adler 1979). Aloneness as an experienced affect is timeless. It is a state that seems always to have been and that will always be; this quality ties it to those moments of life before such organizing categories of thought as futurity and past have been developed. Noteworthy also is the eerie quality of the aloneness experience; it is often accompanied by some sense of unreality, explicable perhaps in terms of depersonalization, but also as a regressive affective hearkening back to the time when self-object differentiation was incomplete and the mother's failure to respond was experienced as though some vital aspect of the inchoate self were hideously missing. Aloneness has the quality of unreal emptiness. Finally, the parallel between the danger reaction of primary anxiety and the nameless horror that accompanies adult states of aloneness may be mentioned, because those in the grips of such reactions will often say that they feel they are dying.

In normal development inside the empathically secure, structure-promoting envelope with its mother, the small child re-experiences the following cycle thousands of times. Anxiety rises. The child gives his mother a danger signal and the mother responds with appropriate comforting activity. Anxiety wanes. In this way tension relief becomes tied to the anxiety signal, and so does the hopeful expectation of relief. The reasonably competent mother is able to prevent the repetition of too many traumatic situations in her child, while at the same time allowing him more frequent experiences of separation as he gradually acquires from her the capacity to tolerate it. This capacity, according to some theorists, develops by a process of "transmuting internalization." When a tolerable, phase-appropriate loss of some discrete function the mother carries out for the child takes place (in this case, anxiety regulation), the child's mind does not resign itself to the loss, but preserves the function by internalizing it, thereby producing a transmutation in the structure of its own self. The child develops an increased capacity to do for itself what once its mother did (Kohut 1971). In effect, it has been argued that the child experiences a kind of signal anxiety as soon as it manages to establish a harmonious rapport with its mother. He experiences anxiety and sends a distress signal; she responds with soothing, protecting him from excessive tension build-up, while at the same time permitting such degrees of separation as the child can tolerate without too much discomfort. The signal anxiety function becomes a part of the maturing child's ego as thousands of appropriate little separation experiences result in a lasting structure built up from transmuting internalizations (Tolpin 1971). Ultimately the early stirrings of anxiety will signal incipient danger, but relief is possible and expected, if not always from mother, then from the child's own neuromuscular activity. He has acquired the emotional disposition to relieve tension by organizing some action of his own in the direction of others whom he trusts to respond in a helpful way. Finally, under most circumstances, the child will have internalized enough of the mother's soothing functions so that he can quiet himself automatically without having to seek out mother or others in times of solitude.

There is a second intolerable affect, *suicidal worthlessness*, closely related to the first, *aloneness,* as a subjective experience and as a pathological development. The subjective experience of utter worthlessness is related to the experience of aloneness and cannot be entirely separated from it because both threaten, or even announce, irrevocable abandonment. In the grips of aloneness the patient is convinced he will be forever cut off from the possibility of human connectedness; in suicidal worthlessness, the patient is convinced he can never merit the caring notice of anyone, including himself, again. The subjective result is very much the same; to be beyond love is to be hopelessly alone. To this observation we will return in a few pages.

The sense of being beyond love is only one aspect of suicidal worthlessness. There is an additional aspect to this affect—the experience of intense and relentless self-contempt. The deeper understanding of these self-attributes will require an excursion into the terrain of the superego and its work in the regulation of self-respect.

We have seen how structures necessary for anxiety regulation are assigned by psychoanalytic theory to the ego, and that what is internalized there are transmuting precipitates of soothing maternal functions, taken in bit by bit, mostly by identification. It is not the whole person of the mother who has been taken in, but rather functions which derive from her. When an adult quiets himself down, therefore, he has no subjective inner sense that he is being aided in his task by something he has learned from anyone else; no inner mother seems to stand nearby speaking calm assurances that all will be well. It seems to the anxious individual that he copes adequately from his own mental resources. This state of affairs prevails because his capacities in this regard are based on *ego identifications.* The adult's mental capacity for coping with anxiety is not linked to a mental representation of his mother as a whole person (a composite mental picture built up over time), but to a mental representation of the adult himself, i.e., his self representation. This is so because a substantial degree of the functional internalizing took place before the child was able to evoke a whole object representation in his mind, before he had a well-established sense that he was a separate person from his mother.

The regulation of self-esteem is subjectively a different experience, especially in the matter of self-criticism. Sometimes the experience of guilt is like getting caught red-handed in some misdeed and being hauled up before an interior judge. The scolding one receives does not feel as though it comes from the mind and heart of the central self; it seems to come from another source (person) contained, however uncomfortably, elsewhere within the confines of one's mind. This reminds us that in subjective experience there are areas of the mind which do not quite belong to the core of the self. In normal individuals this zone (it is part of the "inner world" in Hartmann's language) is inhabited by mental representations of other people, and especially by that watching presence, the conscience (Hartmann 1939; Sandler 1962). The German word for superego is very suggestive of what life within the mind is like for many people who are not comfortably "at home" with conscience— it is *das Über-ich*, translatable (with a little license) as the "over me." The experience of being watched by conscience is often quite painful for sicker patients whose self-critical faculty is very aggressive and very unforgiving. Their guilty inner life is subjectively akin to that of persons afflicted with paranoid delusions. Both feel persecuted and victimized, one from within, the other, from without.

As soon as the child is able to form mental representations of his parents as separate people he begins to organize a more or less integrated schema that will, with the passing of the Oedipus complex, become introjected as his superego. That is to say, the schema will be substituted for the parents as the principal source of self-estimation. In post-Oedipal regulation of self-esteem, the superego takes over a function that formerly belonged to the parents (Sandler 1960). Thus it is that what was once experienced as criticism from the outside becomes criticism from the inside.

Because the introjection which leads to superego formation takes place well after the child has acquired the capacity to tell the difference between himself and others as separate individuals, and because the introjects are formed from whole object representations, the conscience is apt to be felt ever after as separate from and possibly "over" the core of the self, just as the parents were. As the superego is formed, intense aggressive and erotic impulses originally attributed to the parents are bound up and carried inside, remaining attached to the introjected parent-representing schema. This probably accounts for its tendency to manifest itself in the inner world as a sometimes unfriendly, occasionally dangerous, denizen.

The superego in suicidal individuals is severely aggressive. Many of them were neglected as children, deprived of consistent empathic contact and often physically and emotionally abused. Repeated frustration of emotional needs arouses great hostility, and this the suffering child must project onto one or both parents. The parents are often unusually critical or hostile in fact, so that an additional aggressive force is added to the representational schema the child forms of his mother and father. The schema thus formed, exaggerated in its cruelty by the child's projections, may assume ogre-like proportions. Introjection, when it takes place, results in a severe and markedly sadistic superego. Perhaps because the corrective experiences which serve the ordinary child and adolescent to modify the cruelty of the primitive superego are often unavailable, suicide prone individuals do not experience much amelioration of conscience as they approach adulthood. The failure of the superego to soften in adolescence is probably the further consequence of the continuing projection of hostile, critical attitudes onto others. Teachers or other worthy adults are commonly available to growing adolescents. These people are often enough comparatively benign, but if they canot be perceived as such, they cannot be introjected as gentling influences on the superego.

The untamed superego of suicidal patients is therefore implacably critical. They are quick to self-contempt; their consciences are unrelenting and severe, demanding that the patient must pay for every misdeed. The talion code is applied not only for actual misdeeds, but for misdeeds of the patient's imagination and impulse life, conscious and unconscious. Does the patient imagine striking out at his mother? Has he some impulse to do so? "Then strike yourself!" says conscience. Not only mental or physical punishments but self-injuries may be demanded from time to time. Life can bring no mischance or misfortune without a culprit's being sought, and the culprit will commonly be the patient himself.

In this connection can be introduced the third intolerable affect state that plagues these patients, *murderous rage*. States of profound helplessness evoke primitive fight and flight reactions. The patient who suffers from intense experiences of aloneness or self-contempt cannot take flight and is literally backed into a corner, beset by an inescapable and critical superego on the one hand, by anxiety of unmasterable proportions on the other.

Children in a separation panic are often observed not only to be terrified, but to react with fury when their mothers threaten to go away. Suicide vulnerable patients, not having mastered the developmental task of separation, remain vulnerable to regressive attacks of murderous hostility in adult life when losses are threatened. Under such circumstances states of fury may develop that last for weeks and months, making rest impossible; there may be a danger of murder. In fact, homicide followed by suicide commonly takes place when an unendurable loss is threatened. Murder-suicide sometimes occurs in the context of marital breakup.

Sometimes the patient will kill himself in order to avoid murdering someone else; sensing a weakening of self-control, he destroys himself in order to protect another. Intense guilt may also supervene because of murderous impulses, and because of the severity of the patient's conscience, suicide may be demanded as a punishment.

We have considered the critical activities of the superego, experienced subjectively like an interior demon, revealing its origins in the parents from which it sprang. Let us turn our attention to another superego function, that of caring for and protecting the self. Most of Freud's discussion of the superego concentrated on its critical functions. He specifically indicated that the destructive energies of the Oedipal child's relationships with his parents were bound up in the superego, the libidinal ones in the ego, as introjection and instinctual differentiation took place (Freud 1923). This division of energies he never treated as absolute, however, and subsequently, he repeatedly ascribed caring and protective attitudes to the superego (Freud 1938). Schafer (1960) has very usefully surveyed and summarized this important and often overlooked aspect of superego function.

Suicidal patients are quite commonly indifferent to their physical welfare, ignoring the fact that they are uncomfortable, hungry, or cold. They may feel these sensations in the ordinary way, and suffer from them, but they often do not feel the need to take any steps to relieve them. They have little capacity to credit themselves with any worth; rarely if ever do they feel the warmth of even the briefest self-congratulation. They are unable to give themselves any love. The superego fails to invest the ego (self) with narcissistic libido even when the patient attains some approximation to the superego's expectations.

Cases of this sort suggest that the parent representations introjected in superego formation were ungenerous and unloving to the child, or that satisfactory introjection of a loving superego did not take place, because the child was unable to develop a preintrojective superego schema which included representations of parents who loved, who noticed, and who admired him in appropriate ways. This state of affairs might be expected to arise when parents are in fact emotionally uninterested in a child, in cases of traumatic disruptions of parent-child relationships at developmentally critical times, in instances wherein the child's distortions of his actual parents resulted in the development of unloving parent representations, or in the event the child is unable for biochemical or other reasons to complete the task of introjecting a loving superego.

We can better understand this problem by examining an unloving mother representation borrowed from a fairy tale. Hans Christian Andersen (1935) provides an example in the beloved, beautiful witch of his story, "The Snow Queen." The protagonist of the tale, a little boy named Kay, gets fragments of an evil mirror into his eye and heart while playing one day. This mirror, the creation of a wicked magician, had the peculiarity that "everything good and beautiful, when reflected in it, shrank up to almost nothing whilst those things that were ugly and useless were magnified, and made to appear ten times worse than before."

As a result of this misfortune Kay falls under the enchantment of the Snow Queen. She seems exquisitely fair and delicate to Kay, a lady dressed in the finest white crêpe and fur, her attire composed of millions of star-like particles. But she is made entirely of ice and she has no love. The Snow Queen steals Kay away with her to the far North, but he feels no danger. She seems perfect to him, although in her presence he feels little and inferior and reflects that he does not know very much. In her dreary palace poor Kay grows blue with cold. She sets him to arranging sharp ice fragments together to spell words. The Snow Queen, encouraging aspirations to omnipotence, tells him that when he can contrive to form the word "Eternity" from the fragments of ice he shall be his own master and she will give him the whole world, but of course the task is impossible, and he always fails. In time he is rescued by the loving warmth of a little girl, Gerda, his former playmate, whose tears melt Kay's frozen heart and wash away the evil fragments of the mirror.

Patients in the grip of a loveless superego which demands the impossible may figuratively be said to freeze to death because they are deprived of narcissistic warmth. Aspiring after an omnipotent perfect self-ideal, they are unable to see that their quest is hopeless, that what they pursue so devotedly is really a chimera whose quest condemns them to a life of self-indifference at best. Such patients may feel themselves to be so insignificant, so poor in worth, that they do not feel worth taking care of, and will not take care of themselves. Emotionally they are in danger of withering out of self-neglect, and they may do so, unless someone intervenes from outside.

What we encounter in clinical practice, of course, are patients whose superegos are at once profoundly critical and at the same time quite unloving. In consequence the suicidal patient is not only self-contemptuous, but at the same time, self-indifferent. His conscience at once resembles an ogre and the Snow Queen, and against such an inner enemy, the self may be extremely hard-pressed to survive without external help.

At the beginning of this chapter despair was said to have two components: intolerable suffering (aloneness, murderous hate, and self-contempt) and an experience of "recognition" in which the patient gives up on himself.

A common phenomenon in deeply depressed patients is a fear of death. Indeed, when such a patient begins to worry that he might die, the clinician should be alert to the evolution of a suicidal crisis. There is but a short step from melancholic death fears to lethal despair. Freud (1923) commented,

The fear of death in melancholia only admits of one explanation: that the ego gives itself up because it feels itself hated and persecuted by the super-ego, instead of loved. To the ego, therefore, living means the same as being loved—being loved by the super-ego, which here again appears as the representative of the id. The super-ego fulfills the same function of protecting and saving that was fulfilled in earlier days by the father and later by Providence or Destiny. But, when the ego finds itself in an excessive real danger which it believes itself unable to overcome by its own strength, it is bound to draw the same conclusion. It sees itself deserted by all protecting forces and lets itself die.

Does the intolerable distress that finally overwhelms the ego come first, leading then to the surrender of hope (Freud's abandonment of the ego by the superego), or are the experiences of aloneness, self-contempt, and murderous hate not themselves the consequence of incipient superego abandonment? In any case it would appear that intense, prolonged states of helpless mental suffering are not consistent with continuing narcissistic stability, and that self-survival in the long run requires the capacity to escape from intense pain.

If the ego of a suicide-vulnerable person is loosely organized and susceptible to regressions under stress, and if his superego is cruel and unloving, it remains only to add that his instinctual responses are typically intensely colored by aggression. Masochistic and sadistic fixations are usual in these patients, deriving from the same developmental period in which so much difficulty with separation is likely to occur—roughly speaking, between the first and fifth years. These patients are cruel to themselves and cruel to others; they elicit malicious responses from those with whom they become emotionally involved. Early struggles with their mothers are repeated with others in later life. They seek suffering, and they evoke it. Of course this difficulty makes lasting and sustained relationships with others difficult.

Sustaining Resources

Those unfortunate people who reach adulthood without having developed sufficiently stable self-regulatory structures remain vulnerable to crises of aloneness, self-contempt, and fury that may bring about suicide, or dangerous suicidal attempts. In order to minimize emotional distress they must rely on such resources as they can find outside themselves, since they lack anything adequate inside to accomplish the task. There are three categories of such non-structural exterior resources: relationships to others, relationships to work, and relationships to self-parts.

One cannot overestimate the importance of these external sources of comfort and valuing. They stand between the patient and unendurable affects which can drive him to suicide.

In a previous discussion of this subject Buie and I (1983) adopted a term of Kohut's (1971) to denote all classes of these sustaining resources: self-object. We defined it as "any person or other external resource that functions to maintain self integrity which the mature self can do unassisted." Those readers who find the term helpful are welcome to it; for purposes of clarity, however, I have decided to abandon it, inasmuch as some of the sustaining resources about to be discussed are not other persons (objects) at all. Others, while part of the self, do not belong to the core of the self. They nevertheless are necessary for self-regulation, and are closer to the superego, or introjective realm, than to the ego.

In the course of the clinical teaching for which he was famous, Elvin Semrad used to refer to some patients as "love addicts," prone to develop symptoms of "withdrawal" when the love of sustaining others was lost. Literature provides many such examples—young Werther, for example, who, deprived of the love of Lotte, with whom he was infatuated, put a bullet through his head (Goethe 1774), or poor Blanche DuBois in *A Streetcar Named Desire* who in order to maintain her mental balance had "always depended on the kindness of strangers." (Williams 1947). Maugham's *Of Human Bondage* (1915) portrays the helpless erotic dependency of young Philip on a prostitute named Mildred. Those patients who are unable to tolerate solitude and who require exterior buttressing in order to sustain self-regard can grow slavishly dependent on someone else, idealizing the supporting other person, and clinging tight in the way that a frightened, lonely child may cling to his mother when he fears she may go away. These unfortunate patients tend to want an exclusive relationship with their supporting other, unconsciously fearing that any sharing is a prelude to abandonment. Many are pathologically jealous; their aggressively dependent, demanding behavior can make them repellent, so that they repeatedly provoke the loss they most fear. Others nestle quietly into the supportive relationship and are able to function fairly well until a loss is threatened, showing no sign of suicidal regression until that time.

Case 1. A 43-year-old woman lost her husband and only daughter in an automobile accident. During the night after the funeral she overdosed, spent four days in a coma, and subsequently went to live with her in-laws. She made another attempt, was rehospitalized, and announced her intention to keep on trying until she succeeded. After extensive further treatment she was discharged to her family and a few weeks later succeeded in committing suicide, as she had said she would. (cited by Baechler 1975:84)

Loss suicides of this sort are extremely common, and likely to take place in the context of divorce or threatened marital breakup. Alcoholics are particularly likely to commit suicide in the context of loss.

Case 2. A 31-year-old service station worker grew increasingly irritable after he discovered that his wife was having an affair with another man. In response to his discovery he assaulted her and began to threaten suicide. When she asked him for a divorce he refused because, he said, he loved her too much; he told his mother-in-law "I can't live without her." On the night of his suicide he had been drinking while his wife rested. He went into her room and said, "I'm going to settle this once and for all. I'm going to bring him [the lover] here." Over her objections he did so, intending to force a final choice between the lover and himself; a violent argument ensued. The patient pulled a knife, stabbed his wife, stabbed the other man six times and them stabbed himself to death. (Robins 1981:236)

In the cases described, lasting attachment to sustaining others is plainly implied, but in many instances those upon whom the patient depends may be fairly readily interchangeable; one friend or lover is readily substituted for another. In narcissistic object choice the full nature and character of the other person is not so much what is loved; it is what the other person provides that matters. Unable to soothe and value himself, the suicide vulnerable person may require no more of someone else than the provision of soothing and loving. Once he receives what he requires, the patient busies himself elsewhere, showing little other interest in the person on whom he depends.

So marked is this characteristic in some patients that they require no more than seemingly casual (if vital) occasional phys-ical satisfactions obtained from a succession of strangers, of whom nothing more is asked than the provision of a meal or sexual contact. What we have here are not complete object relationships, but relationships to part-objects, a pathological perseverence into adult life of the small child's relating to parts of its mother's body as gratifying, comfort-giving zones before she was fully recognized as a total, separate person. Some suicidal patients can keep themselves in some kind of equilibrium through sexually promiscuous contact with a variety of strangers.

Although the term *part-object* is associated in the minds of many with the Kleinian school, and though it does not occur in Freud's vocabulary, it was in fact an early coinage of the psychoanalytic pioneer Karl Abraham (1924). There we find the proposition that the small child, not yet quite aware of its mother as a separate being, is not yet capable of relating to her as a whole separate person. The earliest stages of object love are characterized, rather, by the discovery that certain organs that afford gratification (tension relief) have a quality of sepa-rateness. A child at this age is capable of part love, not mature object love, and that part which is the object of his emotional interest is the part-object. Later theorists argued that as the child abandoned the parental organs as libidinal objects when the capacity for whole object relationships appeared and maturation progressed, introjection of the part-objects would take place (Glover 1930). The role of the part-object introjects in the development of the capacity to master anxiety is to form early nuclei of mental structures to ward off automatic (traumatic) anxiety and to prevent later psychotic regression. Not in ordinary homosexuals whose relationships to their partners imply the capacity to form whole-object attachments, however narcissistic, but in certain others, the partner is thought of and experienced not as a real, complete person, but as one or more highly exciting organs webbed together by a mass of uninteresting other tissues. There is an intense idealization of some body part, and it is contact with the part, not the other person, which is so imperiously interesting. The same may be said of some heterosexually promiscuous men. The implication is that the part-object introjected in early childhood can be projected later onto the corresponding body part of other adults, and that by tension discharge with the part-object thus recreated in illusion, greater ego regressions can be avoided in reality testing and in the sphere of relationships to others. Without perverse activity these patients become subject to fury of such intensity that reality testing may be abandoned.

The sustaining exterior resource is not always another person, but may be a pet that the patient endows with human characteristics and uses to soothe anxiety, relying on it for real or imaginary love and affection to alleviate the want of self-love and to soften the burden of self-contempt. Baechler (1975:86) records the case of a lonely, sick old man who hanged himself in a psychiatric institution after the cat who lived there died. Borderline and schizophrenic patients are often able to make sufficiently satisfactory reality distortions so that a pet may seem like a steady, admiring, and loving partner. Other people may come and go, but the pet endures. Animals do not have long lives, but some of these patients solve the problem of pet loss by imagining that the soul of the lost pet transmigrates into that of another of the same species. Thus the patient avoids the problem that the death of a beloved tabby might otherwise pose by believing that tabby returns in the form of a new kitten. Not all patients are able to protect themselves with such distortions, however, and the loss of a beloved animal companion can lead to a suicidal crisis.

Case 3. A middle-aged chronically schizophrenic man who was socially isolated but had managed satisfactorily without requiring hospitalization for some months became acutely suicidal and was admitted to a veterans' hospital. There it was learned that his pet canary had died. He felt the bird was his only friend; each day on returning home from work he would watch to see into what part of its cage it would fly; by fluttering from place to place the patient believed his bird was sending him different comments and signals.

Other patients are able to keep up a lively and helpful relationship with certain saints to whom they have a special devotion, feeling protected and watched over by a divine presence, just as some feel continuously in the loving and soothing protective presence of Christ. Others are able to soften the agony that might otherwise follow a loss by convincing themselves that although the person on whom they had depended for soothing and validation has died, the relationship continues from beyond the grave; the husband, the wife, the child, the lover still lingers close by, invisible, to be sure, but a loving and silent presence, although a quiet whisper can sometimes be heard, a light caress can be felt, and visitations can be enjoyed in dreams.

Apart from the patients who must depend on other people, pets, or heavenly friends in order to keep themselves in equilibrium, there are those who idealize a leader, or in some instances, a cause or group devoted to an idealized common end. So long as the leader or the group can be maintained in an idealized form and the patient can feel valued and loved by the leader or others devoted to the same cause, all is well. If something happens to interfere with the idealization, however, or the group or the leader is perceived to repudiate the patient, suicide can occur.

Case 4. Albert Joffe, a devoted communist, was unable to find any meaning in his life after Stalin seized control of the party and turned the Soviet Union in new directions. Before committing suicide Joffe wrote to Trotsky: ". . . when, today, I look at my own past, the twenty-five years I have spent in the ranks of our party, I think I can reasonably say that, for the whole of my conscious life, I have remained faithful to that philosophy. . . . For several years the recent leaders of our party, faithful to their position of not giving members of the opposition any work at all, have accordingly given me nothing whatsoever to do, neither in the area of political policy nor in that of Soviet labor, that corresponds to my talents . . . my health has not ceased to grow worse. . . . That is why it is time to put an end to my life. . . . I cannot go along with a state of affairs where the party tolerates in silence your [Trotsky's] exclusion." (cited by Baechler 1975:85–86)

I have discussed the instances of disappointed idealists such as Joffe here because such people must feel loved and valued by the group to which they dedicate themselves; the group's loving respect seems to serve the same function that the love of another individual would in other circumstances. In normal adulthood satisfactory self-respect arises from comparing oneself with the ideal self held out before one by the superego (ego ideal). When the ego ideal is well established and realistically attainable, self-esteem is typically stable even in the face of losses and disappointment. When the ego ideal has not been satis-factorily developed by normal processes of introjection, however, or when the ego ideal that has been formed is beyond the adult's capacity to achieve, there is a tendency to idealize others, and to idealize causes, as Joffe did. When something happens to injure the exterior idealization, such as the failure of a cause or the ruin of an idealized leader, self-respect may collapse. (Freud 1914)

Work is another kind of sustaining resource that serves to keep some suicide vulnerable patients in satisfactory equilibrium; when the valued work is lost, however, a crisis can supervene. Many who literally live for their work show little interest in others and are virtually without social or intimate relationships. Sometimes it is difficult to decide whether it is the work itself which seems to give the patient a sense of value and quiet, or whether it is the adulation of others who admire his performance. There are probably some people engaged in almost solitary activities who require no more than the work itself. Perhaps for most work-dependent people both work itself and the recognition it compels are important; in any case, most of these patients show little interest in others apart from the applause which they supply.

Case 5. "A sociology professor of sixty became suicidal after a stroke left him almost completely paralyzed on the left side. . . . He became impossibly irritable with his wife and step-children, although he had had a good relationship with them previously. He had grown up with a powerful need for self-sufficiency and control that was fostered by his mother's indifference. A great deal of his self-esteem was tied up with his teaching. He was seen as the best teacher in his department, frequently received accolades for his performance, and was nominated several times for special teaching awards. . . . He had had a recurrent dream during the last five years. He is teaching a class, then begins to move his arms like wings and rises to the top of the room where he flies around the room and then out the window and over some tall trees. He then becomes afraid of the height. In talking about the dream it is clear that he does get 'high' on teaching and on the admiration and awe of his students. His wife had treated him with similar awe and respect. Indeed she continued to do so. His own self-esteem was so tied to receiving admiration for his performance, knowledge, and ability to control situations that he could not conceive of his wife's continuing to love him in his partly disabled condition. . . ." (Hendin, 1981)

Some are little invested in others and care little for their work, and yet are protected from suicide by an intense emotional investment in some particular aspect of their own bodies or minds. They are typically quite indifferent to themselves as persons, and often enough, extremely self critical. One aspect of the self, however, escapes the devaluation, and is highly overprized. As long as this aspect is maintained intact, the patient can maintain his equilibrium, but its loss can provoke a crisis.

Case 6. A middle-aged actuary employed by an insurance company, chronically preoccupied with suicide for many years, and often aware of strong suicidal impulses, managed to survive because of an intense pride in his body. He was without friends, had lost contact with his wife and children since his divorce, and found his work almost unendurably dull. He was, however, an expert swimmer, and extremely vain about his prowess. He spent many hours at his favorite exercise, and liked to admire his body in a full-length mirror. He did not feel he could commit suicide because it would destroy his body and put an end to his swimming. There was nothing else about himself that he felt was worth saving.

Case 7. An aging homosexual restaurateur became acutely suicidal when he developed impotence. He had been highly promiscuous for many years, and though troubled with depression and low self-esteem, he had been able to console himself by admiring his own erections, which he considered formidable, and by attracting the admiring attention of many sexual partners. Nothing else about himself seemed worthwhile, and he was unable to derive any comfort from other people outside a sexual encounter.

The reader might justly object that narcissus-like self invest-ment of the kind encountered in these last two cases really should not be treated as examples of reliance on exterior sustaining resources. The resources depended upon are really body functions of the patients themselves, and therefore hardly exterior. In reply I can only say that a patient of this sort does not experience the overvalued self-part as belonging to the core of himself, but as something rather outside it. The core self is felt to be comparatively worthless. The overvalued part is felt to be an appurtenance of the self and is treasured in the way a precious possession would be. The actuary could be said to be in love not with himself, but with his swimmer's body; the restaurateur, not with himself, but with his penis. In these cases the beloved self-part stands between the self and others, as subjectively experienced, and does not seem to belong quite to the self, though it clearly does not belong to others either. It belongs to an intermediate zone.

Obviously what is being described here is the persistence into adult life of Winnicott's transitional object phenomenon. Some children choose a favorite possession, such as a blanket, as an external comforter while in the process of building up soothing and self-valuing inner structures through internalizing the mother. Some children use body parts such as the thumb or an ear lobe for such a purpose. It is perfectly reasonable to suppose that when these internalizations fail, transitional object phenomena may persist into adult life. Clinical experience proves the expectation. The use of body parts and functions for consolation is by no means unusual in suicide vulnerable in-dividuals, many of whom suffer from borderline personality disorders. Festishes can indicate the persistence into adult life of treasured transitional objects from childhood, usually trans-formed but sometimes almost unchanged.

In passing it is worth noticing that those patients who main-tain their equilibrium by relying on heavenly presences and

those who endow their pets with comforting human characteristics are making creative use of the same intermediate zone
of imaginative illusion. "This intermediate area of experience,
unchallenged in respect of its belonging to inner or external
(shared) reality, constitutes the greater part of the infant's experience and throughout life is retained in the intense experiencing that belongs to the arts and to religion and to imaginative living, and to creative scientific work." (Winnicott 1953)

As we have seen, a suicidal crisis is likely to develop when
a vulnerable individual is deprived of the sustaining resource
necessary for the preservation of emotional equilibrium. An
attempt at suicide is likely to take place unless the patient
succeeds either in recovering the sustaining resource that has
been lost, or in substituting another one for it.

The so-called "cry for help" that suicide threats and attempts
often represent can be understood as bids to obtain such a
substitute resource; in almost all cases, it is another person who
is sought. Suicidal individuals are commonly very fastidious,
however, in what they will accept as substitute resources. Some
will reject a sustaining relationship with any person other than
the one who has been lost, and others, especially those sustained
solely by work or some self-aspect, may reject all relationships.
In such circumstances management of the crisis can be difficult
and longer periods of hospital care may be necessary.

Some patients can avoid a crisis of aloneness, self-hate, and
fury through denial and distortion. In the most extreme instances delusions may appear, barriers to ward off the painful
affect that acknowledgement of loss would entail.

Case 8. A woman in her middle thirties had, after a long courtship,
become engaged to be married to a man who was almost her only
friend. He broke off the wedding plans at the very last minute; the
disappointed bride developed a fixed delusion that he would reappear
at any moment and that the marriage would soon go forward.

Other patients may develop delusions that they are beloved by others who in fact have little if any relationship with them at all. Small indications of politeness or friendly regard may be grossly distorted, enabling the patient to believe that secret signals of undying, passionate love are being given (De Clerambault's Syndrome). Many such patients, unable to find another person to replace a lost, essential external sustaining resource, are forced to create one through psychosis.

Case 9. A chronically depressed and socially isolated teacher, never having recovered from a divorce some years previously, was rejected by a man on whom she had pinned great hopes, and at the same time, lost a close friend who moved to a different part of the country. After some weeks of deepening depression her mood lifted; she developed the delusion that the principal of the school in which she was teaching, a diffident bachelor, was in love with her. She began to make amorous telephone calls and to send love letters that caused great embarrassment.

It may seem strange to treat the capacity for developing delusions as a talent, but the odd fact remains that for vulnerable people otherwise unable to obtain or make use of sustaining resources, psychosis offers the most stable possible protection from intolerable mental anguish and suicide. Schizophrenic and schizoid individuals, who have the greatest difficulty in making and maintaining sustaining relationships with other people, are particularly likely to rely on creative imaginary efforts in order to maintain their equilibrium, sacrificing reality judgment freely as they shape comforting beliefs with the aid of denying and distorting defenses.

Not every patient can develop a fixed delusion that someone else cares, and many must get along with a cherished but precarious illusion that such is so. Others, unable to sustain reasonable self-respect with the aid of inner structures, continue in unsteady balance so long as they can keep up false and grandiose self-illusions. Only when life deals some blow to hope-sustaining dreams will a suicidal crisis apear, warded off previously by the expectation that ultimately the much desired love or success would be realized.

Case 10. A university freshman who had led his class in elementary and secondary school had the reputation in his family and among friends of being an extraordinary genius; he was convinced that he was destined for great things. When he found that he was not brighter than many of his university classmates and that the illusion of his genius was not shared by his new teachers, his grandiose dream of being extraordinarily special was shattered and a serious suicide attempt resulted.

Apart from psychosis only one other recourse remains open for suicide vulnerable people who cannot obtain the necessary sustaining resources if a crisis is to be avoided—chemical relief. This is sometimes obtained in the form of prescribed psychoactive compounds which help mute the intensity of painful affects, and sometimes through recourse to alcohol or other compounds that quite commonly give rise to addictions.

Vulnerability to suicide arises from the failure to develop satisfactory self-regulatory structures in the course of growth. In the absence of these structures, the adult is likely to be overwhelmed with intolerably painful affects that can be warded off only by recourse to sustaining resources—other people, pets, religious faith, reliance on work, or the consolation of some treasured self-aspect. When sustaining resources are not available, or when they are lost, a suicidal crisis will supervene if not avoided by the emergency development of a psychosis or by chemical relief through prescribed medicine, alcohol, or illicit drugging. The nature of the suicide crisis itself is the subject of the next chapter.

2.

The Suicide Crisis

In the preceding chapter we have seen how people who cannot master anxiety and maintain self-regard from within have to rely on sustaining resources from without in order to live from day to day. Deprived of such resources, they fall prey to dangerous affects of worthlessness, aloneness, and homicidal fury—sometimes all three at once. Suicide is then a danger.

Lacking reinforcements from within or without, the patient is thrust into a life-threatening situation; primitive fight responses are called up since flight, except through death, is impossible. If others on whom the patient has depended (or wished to depend) to sustain him seem to threaten abandonment or go away in fact, they invite fury of major proportions. The sustaining person who remains available but who seems unavailable to the patient will be hated with intensity as great as if he were in fact abandoning the patient. Another's failure to meet his vital need, whether in fantasy or in fact, can provoke him to murder.

Should homicidal rage be turned around against the self, suicide may occur, and the other person will be spared. The patient's body often becomes a substitute target of attack because the individual who has sustained him in the past is not only hated but loved. Sometimes the false friend may be out of reach so that killing is impossible. When the failed sustaining resource is not a person but an institution or group instead, killing may again be impossible. Where the predominant motive is to murder a perceived deserter, the patient may waver between suicide and homicide, sometimes committing both.

Suicide for Revenge and Punishment

Would-be suicides often daydream of the guilt and sorrow of others gathered about the coffin, an imaginary spectacle which provides much satisfaction. Zilboorg (1936) has described spite suicides of this sort, commenting that the patients do not necessarily exhibit depressive symptoms, but may be sadistic, cold, and sarcastic. Menninger (1933) noticed that to destroy something dear to another person is an effective means of attack, and that the greatest hurt a mother can endure is to see her child tortured or killed. He pointed out that when a child, piqued at some reproach or denial, takes his own life, he takes it also from his parents. "He robs them of their dearest possession knowing that no other injury could possibly be so painful to them."

Case 11. A twenty-five year old woman, on bad terms with the young man with whom she had been living for some months, enraged after yet another quarrel, drenched herself with eau de cologne and set it afire in order to make her lover sorry for his bad behavior.

Suicide and Murder

Suicidal individuals are obviously profoundly aggressive. Their implacably severe consciences make them profoundly intolerant of their incessant angry impulses; to feel anger of murderous proportions is completely unacceptable (Kernberg 1970) and merits severe punishment. The sustaining person who threatens abandonment is hated, but because he is also loved and often highly idealized, the primitive conscience may demand punishment according to the principle of "an eye for an eye and a tooth for a tooth." The primitive superego forces the aggression around against the self, inexorably sentencing the patient who wishes to kill a beloved person to die by his own hand.

A few may destroy themselves not only to punish themselves, but altruistically, because they sense that their self-control is giving way and that presently, unless some drastic measure is taken, they will commit murder. These suicides are carried out to protect the loved person from what the overwhelmed patient believes, correctly or not, he is about to do.

Suicide is often the equivalent of killing someone else. Freud described this psychology in "Mourning and Melancholia"; the sustaining person who is lost (he referred to an object invested with ego [narcissistic] libido) may be introjected, seeming then to take a place within the person of the patient's own self (ego). Thus it is that the hostility directed at the lost object, often magnified and aroused by the loss, now appears reversed, pointing against the self.

If one listens patiently to a melancholic's many and various self-accusations, one cannot in the end avoid the impression that most often the most violent of them are hardly at all applicable to the patient himself, but that with insignificant modifications they do fit someone else, someone whom the patient loves or has loved or should love. Every time one examines the facts this conjecture is confirmed. So we find the key to the clinical picture: we perceive that the self-reproaches are reproaches against a loved object which have been shifted away from it on to the patient's own ego. (Freud 1917)

The agitated widow of the following case, recently bereaved, exhibited self-reproaches of the kind Freud described. Although she was unknown to him and the available details of her history are scanty, what she says against herself would plainly fit her husband better—he had, after all, "abandoned" her by dying, and according to her beliefs, would be facing the last judgement.

Case 12. A 56-year-old widow, shortly after the death of her husband, began to reproach herself for not having looked after him properly. She developed delusions of sin, claimed her husband had married the devil, that he could not go to heaven, and that she and her children were damned on account of her evil life. She was very restless, sleepless, stopped eating, and persistently lamented, shrieked, and wept. She claimed that she was burning, that she was already in hell, and that she saw her fearful sins in the abyss. She wrote a letter to the authorities begging to be taken to prison and signed it, "Devil." (Kraepelin 1904)

When hate for the introjected person predominates over love, the introject can become a target of physical attack. The fury is turned around against the self, but the subjective experience of the patient is much as though in attacking his own body, he is attacking someone else. The patient's body *becomes* the false friend. That killing it requires self injury is overlooked or denied; destroying the false friend within, who was once without, is more hotly desired than preserving one's own bodily integrity. As we shall see, some patients venture into suicide in the belief that they will not die at all, but that only the hated person will be destroyed.

Observation of suicidal patients repeatedly has shown that gross disturbances in the capacity to discern where the self leaves off and other people begin (self-object differentiation) are commonplace. These patients frequently do not experience mind and body as connected, and subjectively they feel that they are two or more selves, sometimes sequestered together inside the same fleshly envelope, but sometimes not.

The subjective sense of oneself as a continuing individual discrete from others is the complex consequence of a balancing of self and object representations, memories, perceptions, and affects by the ego. It would not appear to depend on the ego or the superego only, but is the result of a dynamic balance of energies, libidinal and aggressive, between ego, superego, and the introjections and identifications which comprise them. This sense of identity implies that the mature ego is able to keep self and object representations separate, and at the same time, to relate them to each other, in fantasy to be sure, but always under the ultimate domination of the reality principle. The sense of self is therefore the subjective, conscious consequence of balanced structures, representations, and affects related to and under the control of the ego.

Jacobson (1964) has suggested that a more precise formulation of the phenomena observed in melancholia would require us to say that the libido and the aggression which are turned back in the direction of the self after object loss are cathected onto the self representation and not onto the system ego at large. She further commented that in psychosis, self and object images become fused in ways that completely disregard realistic differences between the self and the object. Thus it becomes possible for the melancholiac to hate and accuse himself as though he were the ambivalently loved person who has been lost.

The following case illustrates the kind of confusion between self and object to which I refer.

Case 13. The following note was discovered after a 23-year-old patient committed suicide while under hospital treatment. She addressed it to her psychiatrist. "These last few days were a death-like existence. I am so tired I just want to sleep. My mind, oh, my mind, it's sick. I feel as if I am sinking and I can't call for any help but death. I don't seem to feel as though I want to die. It's like another person telling me what to do. I feel as though my mind isn't connected to my body, and it seems to refer to me as 'you,' as in, 'Die, you fool, die.' I feel as though there are two of me, and the killer is winning.

When my death comes, it won't be suicide. It's that someone has murdered me. While I am writing this letter, it's like the other part is laughing at me and calling me a fool for writing this nonsense, but it's how I feel, I know it must sound confusing to you, but this is the only way I can express myself. I wish I could have told you many of my confused feelings, but I feel as though you won't understand and believe me and then the other part takes over and goes into therapy for me. I want to destroy that part of me, but I cannot seem to separate myself in therapy to do it, while it's trying to kill me, I'll kill myself and take it with me. You have done your best to help me, but I just couldn't help myself. I'm so tired I can't fight any more. I wish I could tell someone now, but they can't help me, even worse is they won't understand, oh—if they only would understand, it would mean so much, but nobody has ever understood me so how could I expect someone to now. I took those pills before, it was to kill the other part of me, but I really won't die, I'll just wake up and things will be different. That's how I feel tonight, that I'm not really going to die, and the other one is and I don't know how to explain that to you. I seem to be contradicting myself, but I am writing as I feel. So if you are confused, just think of how I must feel. I have used the term Robot to you, it's like someone is hurt up in my head and is using my eyes as windows and controlling me and my actions. Last week during ward meeting when the people were talking, it was like the voices weren't coming from them and I had to keep looking at their mouths to be sure. I can't even explain that one, it's too hard and you wouldn't understand anyway. I don't know why the hell I'm telling you this anyway, its sounds like a bunch of shit all thrown in together. If you think I'm looking for pity through this, you're crazy, because it won't do me any good, for where I'm going I need pity like I need another problem. Well that's it, so have a good laugh. It's on me." (Maltsberger and Buie 1980)

The patient's subjective self is divided in two; on the one hand, there is the "me" that wants to live, and on the other, the "killer," which the patient experiences as alien to her *self*, but in her *body*. Positioned in her head, it works her body in a robot-like manner. Both the "me" and the "killer" are bent on murder.

The killer as a representation in the patient's inner world does not quite have the quality of an object representation; it is experienced as a part of herself (as a body inhabitant). It must therefore be understood as a component of the self representation even though it is experienced as alien at the same time.

This state of affairs can be explained by the theory that the patient's self representation has, in a suicidal regression, divided into two parts. One portion that the patient calls "me" is the representation of her thinking self, or mind. The other, called "killer," has become associated with the patient's body representation, but the body representation is without qualities of thinking or feeling—it is separated from the representation of the subjective, mental self. "Killer" can be seen as a composite creature that in many respects resembles an external object; it would appear to derive from hostile, ill-integrated introjects. It has been half expelled from the patient's self, and it is highly charged with hate. Having no body of its own, it borrows its corporeity from a portion of the patient's fragmented self representation. The "killer," as it were, steals its physical being from the patient herself. The patient splits off her body representation from her self representation and binds it to the "killer" in order to contrive a physical presence which she may attack. At the same time, the other fragment of the original intact self representation, "me," being divided from the body representation, is experienced as incorporeal, and would therefore seem not to be endangered by the body's destruction; the body has become the domain of the "killer." "Me" set on "killer" in a homicidal attack, as it were, to destroy it before it could destroy her.

Because suicide prone patients are likely to have experienced difficulty in self-object differentiation, they are unusually prone to project their superego attitudes onto others. As a result they commonly believe that others share the scornful self-contempt they direct against themselves. When enough ego regression occurs and reality testing gives way, the superego introjects may assimilate to an object representation, and a paranoid psychosis results. This results in intense persecutory anxiety, but sometimes it protects from suicide, because murderous self hatred is dislocated outwardly and perceived to originate from a delusional exterior enemy.

Thus it is that some patients are able to deal with the intolerable problem of a raging, hateful inner presence like the "killer." In projecting it outward onto others a patient can disavow his own hate and ascribe it to someone else, so that he experiences himself as under attack from the outside. A paranoid psychosis of this sort can be an effective protection from suicide, so long as the patient can maintain it. Such psychoses are often labile, however, especially in middle-aged and elderly patients; when the psychosis abates a suicidal crisis may occur.

Case 14. A recently widowed aging mother of several grown children was admitted to the hospital furiously angry, and markedly deluded with persecutory convictions. These she had developed shortly after the last son who remained at home announced his intention of moving out of the house and getting married. Her psychosis cleared and she was discharged home from the hospital. Afterward she rapidly sank into a depression and surprised everyone by committing suicide.

In this instance the patient was unable to sustain her projections; the angry, critical attitude that she had forced out onto people around her turned around on herself with the clearing of the delusions.

Obviously such individuals as these are subjectively trapped, struggling with a demonic inner enemy, which under some circumstances may be so angry, so cruel, that it issues a death verdict and commands the patient to commit suicide. This will take place unless someone intervenes from the outside.

The development of a paranoid psychosis is not universally protective from suicide, however. While it is, of course, the case that a paranoid psychosis distances the persecuting presence outside the patient, sometimes the chronic experience of being hunted and persecuted from without proves just as intolerable as persecution by the conscience from within. A patient may commit suicide in order to escape from an external delusional persecutor.

Case 15. An unemployed chronic schizophrenic man was admitted under restraints in transfer from a surgical unit. He had impaled himself on a splintered billiard cue and had been saved only by immediate surgical attention. On recovering from the anaesthetic and discovering he was yet alive he lacerated his brachial artery while yet in the recovery room. After he was transferred to the psychiatric service it was learned that the patient had been on a flight from city to city, trying to escape terrifying, persisting hallucinatory voices who condemned and excoriated him. The patient said that he had attempted to kill himself "so I could get under the ground and away from them."

Some patients do not localize the angry presences that plague them in their bodies at large, but limit them to certain zones or organs. The patient described in Case 13 localized the "killer" to her head, though that introject seemed to dominate her whole body. The following case shows how some patients are able to sequester the introjects to certain portions of the self representation, so that a complete sense of alienation from their bodies does not take place.

Case 16. "C. had heard obscene words, which she said her husband often used, in her head for several months. As she entered the acute psychotic state for which her relatives hospitalized her, the words 'moved down into my body'. They moved down gradually over a few hours. 'First into my face, then down into my stomach.' One of the obscene words appeared on her stomach. 'It felt like a monster; felt sick all over.' She described a pain in her stomach at this time. 'My head was very sore and my legs were weak.' Later the bodily sensations disappeared, but the spoken words in her head resumed. It is probable, although not certain, that both were not present at the same time." (Havens 1962)

This woman (she was not suicidal) appeared to make some accommodation to her introjective infestation by hypochondriacal developments. Many borderline people assign certain areas or portions of their bodies to be enemy zones dominated by hostile introjects, commonly derived from their mothers, and these parts are targeted for self-mutilating attacks. They are not always primarily intent on committing suicide—their aim is to injure and assault. Sometimes suicide may result if the patient gets carried away in an angry frenzy and goes too far.

Case 17. A woman in her middle thirties who had never been overtly psychotic complained chronically of feeling empty. She had been prone to cut herself intermittently to relieve a sense of torpor, or deadness. As psychotherapy progressed the patient passed through a phase of profound longing for physical closeness to me, accompanied by active fantasies of incorporating me, either by eating or vaginal entrapment. She was afraid her body might fuse with mine if she came too close, and grew very angry when remembering her mother's lifelong empathic failures to give comfort and understanding. Leaving my consulting room at the end of each session was experienced as a rejection on my part, and she began to linger for half an hour or longer in the washroom. Finally she began to cut herself there. After a number of sessions in which this behavior continued I told the patient that she hated me because she could not make me part of herself, and that she was trying to cut her mother whom she experienced as a bad part of herself. On retiring again to the washroom at the end of the session the patient had a depersonalization experience, and as she opened a shallow cut on her abdomen, she had a strong subjective sense that it was not her own skin she was cutting, but the hated fat belly of her mother. She had something close to but short of an hallucinatory experience. She could perceive the attack was aimed at somebody else, that her abdomen seemed to be the abdomen of somebody else. After that time the cutting soon disappeared.

Many patients with borderline personality disorders suffer from a sense of body alienation that results from the domination of their body representations by hostile introjects. This lies behind much of the depersonalization from which they suffer; it explains why they attack their own skin with sharp objects. One patient told me she felt impelled to cut herself in depersonalized states because her body felt unreal, a marionette, a fake thing that through some trick had been foisted on her.

While I have no case material to prove that a lethal attack against a vital organ can be an effort to destroy an introject which has become identified with the organ, I feel confident that such suicides must occur. Clinical experience has shown self castration can be a symbolic attack against a hated father identified with the patient's genitalia.

There are reports in the literature of suicides occurring at the peak of "homosexual panic," in the absence of an organized delusional system. Furst and Ostow (1979) described the case of a passive young man who was admitted to the hospital after an unprovoked assault on his father. At first the patient developed warm, friendly feelings for his therapist. These unaccountably changed to dislike, then aversion, and finally into the conviction that the therapist was harming, not helping him. When repeated demands for a change of therapist went unheeded and the patient felt unable to escape from the former friend now perceived as an enemy, he panicked, escaped from the hospital, and committed suicide. Paranoid individuals are typically unable to tolerate homosexual impulses and deal with them defensively by turning their erotic longings into their opposite, aversion, which is then projected onto the person who aroused longings for passive surrender in the first place.

Erotic Longing and Suicide

The oral erotic value of suffering and death is often evident when the symbolic meaning of a suicidal act is deciphered. Some patients literally want to be devoured by their mothers. One woman expressed this idea symbolically in the fantasy of being crushed by a subway train; the clatter of the wheels was associated with the sound of gnashing teeth (Arlow 1955). Death by being consumed in flame may have a similar meaning, just as the yawning grave or an abyss may symbolize a mouth opening down into "mother earth."

Water is also a common maternal symbol (the words *wave* and *vulva* come from the same Indo-Germanic root, *vel-*). Symbolization of birth and motherhood by earth and water are commonplace in folklore and occur repeatedly in the dreams and fantasies of everyday life. Since in suicide, as in all death, the body returns to the earth, mixing with it so as to become indistinguishable in the course of time, it is not surprising that for many death is perceived as a means for return to the mother of early infancy, when there was no subjective separateness.

Case 18. Heinrich Wilhelm von Kleist (1777–1811), the German poet and novelist, shot Henriette Vogel, for whom he had a fatal, romantic passion, and then himself, on the shore of the Wannsee near Potsdam in 1811. He was preoccupied with death and suicide, and erotized the grave as a maternal bed. He wrote, "I must confess to you that her grave is dearer to me than the beds of all the empresses of the world." The empress, like queen, is a well-known unconscious symbol of the mother. Toward Henriette he displayed a passionate tenderness, rapturously exchanging pet names with her in a final outburst. (Jones 1911)

Pain, suffering and helplessness are sometimes erotized; elaborate sexual rituals may evolve in which torture, hanging and asphyxiation lead to orgasm at the point where death seems imminent (Resnick 1972). Death sometimes indeed takes place in these circumstances. Litman and Swearingen (1972) described a patient who achieved orgasm by being choked unconscious; he liked to imagine a situation he associated with death and dying: being abandoned while tied up and locked in a small box, obviously symbolic of a coffin.

The craving for punishment in association with sexual activity is frequently associated with guilt for incestuous wishes. Psychoanalytic study of a high proportion of patients reveals minor masochistic trends in adolescent masturbatory fantasies, wherein intercourse is permitted only if some punishment is inflicted. More deeply pathological patients may personify death as an Oedipal lover, so that the punishment of execution is imposed at the moment of imaginary incest.

Psychoanalysis attributes the fragmentation of the self representation, the splitting off of its various parts, and their confusion with part or whole object representations to regression in ego functioning. We have been discussing, of course, the loss of the capacity to maintain self and object differentiation, normally well established before the advent of the Oedipal phase of development. There is another ego regression which must now claim our attention; it, too, plays a major part in the development of suicidal crises. I refer to the loss of the capacity for reality testing, or the capacity to distinguish between fantasy and reality.

Death Fantasies

Suicidal individuals are likely to entertain a number of illusions and delusions concerning the nature of death. Among these are the belief that death is a state of "nothingness," by which they ordinarily mean peaceful rest, the belief that death can lead to rebirth in a better world, and the belief that death can lead to the recovery of losses.

Many patients contemplating suicide will, when asked what they imagine it would be like to "be" dead, reply that in death they would "be nothing." Close examination of the clinical material will usually reveal that there is a fantasy that life, however transformed, will nevertheless continue in a better, more peaceful way, beyond the grave.

Nothing is after all no more than a term of negation, implying the absence of matter, time, and space. When a patient expresses the fantasy that he will through death *become* nothing, or *arrive* at nothing, we cannot rest with the manifest statement, but look instead to the unconscious meaning he attributes to such a state. There is, of course, no such *state*; a state implies being. What are the components of so-called nothingness? It can be defined as the conglomerate of the negatives of daily experience, and these are four:

1. The opposite of perceptive capacity is insentience.
2. The opposite of consciousness is unconsciousness.
3. The opposite of physical being is incorporeity.
4. The opposite of having a place in the stream of time is timelessness.

These negatives taken together will allow us to define the imaginary state of nothingness as a state of insensate, unconscious, bodiless timelessness. But nothingness so conceived remains nevertheless a *state of being*.

When somebody begins to long actively to "become nothing" one may reasonably assume that the abstraction of nothingness has taken on a symbolic meaning, and that some components of the abstraction have become equated with the aim of an unconscious drive. That a drive operates we may be sure because pseudonothingness is desired, and behind desire lie the instincts. Sometimes the desire is clinically observed in the form of a deep, nostalgic yearning. At other times, desire is expressed in terms of surcease from pain; but however expressed, some balancing and weighing of life and death on the scales of pleasure-unpleasure is always detectable.

If the desire is investigated the clinician will often find that the patient craves the restful oblivion of peaceful sleep. Sleep, of course, has nothing to do with death. The tendency to equate death with sleep is nevertheless both ancient and universal. The Greeks believed that Hypnos, the god of sleep, and Thanatos, god of death, were brothers. Literature is filled with such allusions. Keats's sonnet "To Sleep" calls upon the "embalmer" of midnight to "seal the casket of my soul" so that he may escape from a burrowing, mole-like conscience.

While nothingness as an experience is beyond our ken, the oblivion of easeful rest is known to all. It belongs to some of the sleep of adulthood, but more to the sleep of children. Pleasant oblivion to surroundings, to perception, to time, to separateness from the great world outside and the others who populate it is the experience of a sleeping, satiated infant. It seems to me (and to numerous other authors) that this is the state that suicidal patients want to recapture; they only think it is death.

In their inner worlds the self representation tends to fuse with the image of the madonna mother of infancy. By becoming one with her the patient hopes to taste again the omnipotent, timeless, mindless peace of early childhood, away from his wearisome, hostile adult inner world.

Through suicide patients commonly hope to exchange their miserable present plight for another, better life they expect to reach somehow through a passage of death. In its most rudimentary form the better life may be no more than the peaceful rest of "nothingness." Frequently enough, however, the imagined life of the next world is consciously more elaborated.

Case 19. Mr. G., a 63-year-old retired office worker, was transferred to a psychiatric inpatient unit after surviving an almost lethal overdose of digitalis. A former alcoholic, the patient had overcome his difficulties and became well known for his volunteer work. A stroke left him with a thalamic infarction. He experienced great difficulty in urinating. Frequent catheterization became necessary and his leg brace was commonly wet with urine. The stroke left him subject to severe attacks of pain in which his hand, arm and leg felt as though they were being crushed in a vise or pierced with sharp needles—the worst experiences of pain in his entire life. Further, his ailments forced him out of the home he had shared for some years with friends. What he ostensibly found intolerable was physical decay and the suffering for which he could find no relief. He had hoarded digitalis, planning to commit suicide for years, promising himself "escape" when the suffering became too much. But careful examination showed that in fact what made it intolerable was the loss of his pet dog "Fidel."

When asked what he had imagined it would be like to be dead, Mr. G. began to cry, and confided that he had hoped Fidel would be there "on the other side" waiting for him. He was careful to point out he had no sense of certainty, but a strong hope, about life beyond the grave. The patient told the examiner about Fidel eagerly, in great detail, weeping all the while as he explained how inseparable they had been. Fidel accompanied him to banquets, appeared on the platform with him, had attracted the notice of celebrities. For years Mr. G. had secretly smuggled Fidel into movies. His intelligence had been noted by everyone; the patient and his pet had enjoyed a complete mutual capacity to understand each others' thoughts and feelings. They were the closest of friends.

When Fidel was 13 years old "he developed diabetes and required insulin injections"; urinary incontinence followed. On the advice of the veterinarian the dog was given "euthanasia." After cremation his ashes were dispersed on a beach where "by coincidence" those of a friend's wife had been scattered before. Mr. G. liked to imagine that she and Fidel were keeping each other company.

Before this hospitalization the patient had not seen the connection between Fidel's illness and "euthanasia" and his own incontinence and suicide attempt.

Mr. G.'s mother had been physically and emotionally abusive; he had relied on his father and brother to raise him. From the age of 14 he was never without a dog and earlier would leave for school a half hour early in order to "have conversations with four dogs who lived in the neighborhood." When asked if he would have attempted suicide had Fidel remained at his side Mr. G. exclaimed indignantly, "What? Leave Fidel? Never!"

In this case it is obvious that the patient had a life-long reliance on dogs as sustaining resources, not having developed interior structures to help ward off the affects of despair. Having lost his dog, the patient actually believed that his equilibrium might be restored by recovering the pet through suicide.

Typically a death-fantasy in suicidal cases involves several of the following components: 1) Death is seen as an escape from intolerable affects in the present. 2) Death is seen as a journey. Freud (1900:254), of course, called attention to the fact that children conceive of death as a "going away," a journey. The connection between death and travel is archaic, as is the connection between death and sleep. Teutonic and Greek mythology tell of processions of dead souls, and Hamlet refers to that "undiscovered country, from whose bourn no traveller returns." (Jenson 1958) 3) Death is a means of achieving a reunion with a beloved other, typically through fusion (becoming "nothing" with the primaeval mother), but not always, as in the case of Mr. G. 4) Death is not imagined as a cessation, but as a personal transformation.

While some patients may commit suicide under the influence of frank delusions—their death-fantasies are not hopes, but fixed convictions that remain unshakeable—many others do so under the sway of death-illusions that have great emotional intensity. Mr. G. was not certain that he would be reunited with Fidel in dying, but his life had become so discouraging, so impoverished, had lost so much of its value, that the fantasy of being reunited with his dog was prized more greatly than his impoverished reality. The fantasy seemed so much finer that he was prepared to make a lethal gamble. He said that he was not certain, but that he hoped. Under stressful circumstances, illusions of this sort can operate with all the force of a delusion, and they are particularly likely to play a dangerous role in those patients whose capacity to distinguish between wish and reality is tenuous under ordinary circumstances.

Suicidal crises can be expected to appear in those patients who lack the necessary structure to protect themselves from the intolerable affects of suicide (aloneness, self contempt, murderous hate) and who must rely on sustaining resources outside themselves to maintain equilibrium. A crisis will develop when the sustaining resource fails.

Under such circumstances the patient will be thrown into a state of intolerable emotional pain. Regressions in ego functioning then take place, with confusions about body boundaries, and misperceptions that parts of the self belong to others. Withdrawal of emotional investment in the painful real world is commonly followed by the building up of latent fantasies concerning death into powerful wishes that may become delusions or operate with delusional force (object libido is withdrawn and becomes attached to the ego, transformed into secondary narcissistic libido). The capacity to recognize and respect the difference between reality and death fantasy may fail, and suicide can result.

3.

Recognizing the Suicidal Patient

So massive is the suicide literature that any attempt to master it may stagger not only the mind, but the back as well. The abstracts alone of articles printed in English for the past ten years weighed more than eight pounds when the paper on which they were printed was laid on the scales at the corner grocery. Forests are destroyed to feed the whirring presses; many new articles and a book or two appear each month. A substantial number of these are statistical surveys dealing with diagnostic, social, or biographical characteristics of patients who attempt or succeed at suicide. There are sociological studies, too, and epidemiological, psychoanalytic, neurochemical, genetic, therapeutic ones. They pour from suicide research centers, medical schools and hospitals, and university departments of psychology and sociology, often spilling over into the popular press. That so many expend so much effort with this difficult subject is well, for suicide, after accidents, is the leading cause of death in young adults.

The clinician, confronted with a distressed patient who may or may not commit suicide, must form the best judgment of risk he can in order to plan a reasonable course of treatment. From the plethora of published material, from what can he draw to help him recognize a suicidal patient when he meets one? The answer to that question is obviously the principal subject of this book; in answer to it, let us begin with a survey of the different approaches to the problem to see what each has to offer. Statistical studies are helpful, especially when special subpopulations are studied; diagnosis alerts us. Psychological testing can lend valuable aid; from the research laboratory comes word of a neurochemical test specific for patients at high suicide risk. Those who decide about suicide danger on the basis of clinical intuition or the mental state examination alone are likely to make dangerous errors. Psychodynamic case formulation, the estimation of suicide danger based on a psychoanalytic understanding of the patient's character vulnerability to specific stresses when a crisis arises, is the best means for making clinical decisions on a day to day basis. It is informed by what can be learned from the other methods, but in the long run it relies most heavily on the individual developmental history of each patient and his characteristic ways of responding to stresses, most of which will be losses of one sort or another. Psychodynamic formulation has its deepest roots in the clinical history.

Predicting suicide at present is an insuperable task. We cannot do it. The challenge to identify those who at some time in the future will commit suicide is essentially a statistical one—the difficulties are immense. Suicide remains a comparatively rare event; as case frequency diminishes, prediction becomes more uncertain because of the decreasing probability that any given case will be positive (Murphy 1985). Statistical methods will identify high risk groups readily enough, and that is a valuable aid. But they cannot do more; selecting the particular patient in the high risk group who is sure to commit suicide is beyond this approach. Absolute prediction is impossible by any method. Alerted by known probabilities, however, the clinician may make informed judgments about individual patients in the high risk group with the help of psychodynamic formulation.

The suicide rate in the United States has been increasing gradually over the past twenty years. In 1960, the general suicide rate (the number of suicides per 100,000 in the population per year) was 10. By 1979, it had risen to 12.4. Although there is considerable alarm in the popular press about increasing rates, the current incidence of suicide remains substantially below that of the Depression years. In 1933 the rate was 15.9. Suicide rates tend to be high in times of economic depression and low when the country is at war—it was 9.5 in 1944.

Any inspection of total population suicide rates is likely to be misleading because about two thirds of the suicides in any given year are white males; overall population rates will be skewed, therefore, by the characteristics of the white male group. Women attempt suicide more often than men do, but among completed suicides, there are two or three males for every female.

Another consistent pattern is this—the suicide rates of white males tend to increase directly with age with the highest rates being found among the elderly. The rates for white females increase until the ages of 45–64, and then decrease slightly. The age patterns of nonwhites reach their highest points in the 25–34 year age groups and then tend to decline or remain level. Clinicians will do well to bear in mind that when the overall population is reviewed, *aging white males are at the greatest suicide risk of all.* The suicide rate for white men over the age of 45 rises rapidly, soon exceeding 40 per 100,000, and reaching 78 in old age (85 or above).

Adolescent suicide rates tripled between 1956 and 1975 (Holinger 1984). While the rate of suicide in white adolescents remains higher than that in blacks (8.9 for whites, 4.4 for blacks in the fifteen to nineteen-year-old group), the suicide rate in black adolescent males is increasing even more rapidly than that in their white cohorts (Frederick 1984). Whereas suicide in whites increases in direct relation to age, it reaches its peak in blacks in youthful years (Davis 1979). If adolescent suicide rates continue to rise as they have done in recent years, they will soon equal those found among older adults. Increasing suicide in young persons, however, has received so much public attention that it is difficult to keep a correct perspective. Suicide rates in young people were at an unusually low point during the early 1950s. If one chooses for a basis of comparison the rate earlier in the century, the increase seen in the 1970s is not so large. Bear in mind also that the suicide rate of young people is quite low, so that an increase of only five suicides per 100,000 would result in a great rate increase among adolescents, even though age patterns in the present rates would remain essentially unchanged (Linden 1976).

One may therefore turn attention elsewhere, leaving overall population patterns aside, acutely sensitized to the danger of suicide in aging white males, alert to the fact that adolescent males, black and white, are at increasing statistical risk and that in general, two or three males will succeed at suicide for every female who does.

Statistical analysis of successful suicides according to diagnostic class is clinically quite helpful; a suicide threat in certain diagnoses is much more alarming than in others. The question of diagnosis as an alerting factor will be discussed more fully in the next chapter; suffice it to say here that patients with major affective disorders comprise half or more of successful suicides. Alcoholics are very suicide vulnerable, and so are schizophrenics, especially when a marked affective (depressive) component is present.

Statistical studies have consistently shown that a variety of findings in the patient's history and social context disposes to suicide. Here is a partial list:

physical illness
history of a previous attempt

recent loss of an important relationship
divorce or separation
never married
suicide of a close relative
abused as a child
homosexuality
living alone
retirement

Notice that a number of these items imply social isolation and the absence of others who under better circumstances might offer emotional support. Other factors indicate circumstances that would make it difficult for a vulnerable adult to maintain himself in a stable way by relying on an exterior sustaining resource.

While each item stands alone as an alerting factor, it is when they occur in combinations in persons who bear high risk diagnoses or who are in a dangerous age group, that substantial risk may be indicated. A 65-year-old white male, recently widowed, and physically unwell is a person at risk. Should he carry a previous diagnosis of major affective illness and be a heavy drinker as well, the situation becomes alarming even before further history is collected.

By the same token a young woman, freshly disappointed in love, but surrounded by a caring family and good friends may make a suicide threat. In the absence of other factors, it is not statistically indicative of great danger.

Nevertheless, many elderly alcoholic physically unwell widowers with a history of depression are not suicidal—some of them are surrounded by loving families and may be managing fairly satisfactorily. Some young women surrounded by supportive others may be plunged into a deep suicidal crisis by losses. Diagnostic and statistical information is useful, in short, because of its alerting function. Standing alone it is insufficient for recognizing a patient at immediate risk for suicide.

Psychological testing is another valuable clinical aid that offers several avenues of study. Projective testing attempts to characterize the patient's inner life. There are two types of rating scale—one is designed to measure the subjective experience of the patient (depression and anxiety scales, for instance); the other, systematically to search out details from the patient about his life experience, objective and subjective, that are known to favor (or dispose against) suicide, weighing each item so that a score of suicidal danger can be obtained.

No psychological test is capable of predicting with any degree of accuracy whether a patient will or will not commit suicide, but certain kinds of responses have been identified in patients who go on to commit suicide, or to carry out lethal attempts. If these findings appear when a given patient is tested, they can be integrated with the rest of the clinical picture in determining the degree of present risk. In the Rorschach examination shaded color responses are found in a large proportion of suicidal patients; in an inkblot the patient combines some comment about chromatic color and shading (i.e., a blue vase standing in the shadow). Human movement responses in which the imagined figures perform an overt act of aggression against each other or against a third person are found more often in Rorschach records where actual instead of attempted suicide has taken place. Human movement responses with animal content are more prominent in suicidal than in nonsuicidal test records (Piotrowski 1968). While Neuringer (1974) was discouraged respecting the utility of the Rorschach for suicide assessment after reviewing the literature, others remain optimistic, especially when combinations of Rorschach signs are looked for. Exner (1977) reported a computer analysis of Rorschach examinations from suicidal patients which identified a constellation of eleven variables, a composit of eight or more of these correctly identifying 75% of the actual suicides in his series and 45% of the attempters. Few false positives among the controls had the same composite.

The Thematic Apperception Test (TAT) was applied to suicidal patients by McEvoy (1963), who found that it did not differentiate between cases with and without suicidal trends. Figure drawing can indicate depression and impulsivity, but not suicide specifically.

Beck's research group has devised a hopelessness scale intended to measure the degree of a given patient's despair. This scale has proven quite helpful in separating suicidally depressed patients from those who are depressed but not suicidal. In fact, through the use of this scale it has been repeatedly shown that suicidal intent does not correlate nearly so closely with depression as it does with hopelessness. (Beck 1974, 1975; Kovacs 1975; Lester 1979; Emery 1981; Wetzel 1976). This hopelessness scale provides a useful adjunct to the mental status examination for clinicians who wish to quantify the degree of patients' despair.

It can be argued that not all patients arrive at suicide by the same route. A set of characteristics might be identified in patients with a history of major depressive disorders which would separate those who were at serious risk for suicide from those who were not, for example. Following this argument Motto (1979) has defined several clinical "models," arguing that for each the process of arriving at a suicidal outcome involves elements unique for each model, and that these elements can indicate psychopathology peculiar to each model in question. A clinical model is comprised of a group of patients who are defined as having certain clinical characteristics in common, alcoholics over the age of fifty, for example, or adopted adolescent girls who make suicide threats. This approach he investigated statistically for two test models (not the random examples I have just suggested for illustration); he demonstrated reliable differences between the models in the distributions of estimated risks for persons who subsequently committed suicide compared with those who did not. This study paved the way for the preparation of useful psychological tests of the second sort mentioned—sophisticated scales in which various factors in the patient's biography and subjective experience can be weighted and the patient assigned a numerical score to indicate level of suicide risk.

A suicide risk scale was next developed for the model of patients hospitalized due to a depressive or suicidal state. Some 2,753 such subjects were prospectively studied regarding 101 psychosocial variables. In a two year followup 136 of these subjects were dead of suicide (5.9 percent). A statistical analysis identified fifteen of the variables as significant predictors of suicidal outcome, and these were developed into a scale, the "risk estimator," which gives an estimated risk of suicide in two years for patients of this kind. This scale has been reproduced in Appendix B.

Motto (1985) comments about the risk estimator scale that it was never the expectation of his group to predict suicide in individual cases; rather they hoped to derive an instrument that would effectively identify patients at substantial risk so as to set these apart for particular clinical attention. The risk estimator scale has not yet been extensively field tested, but it promises to be a robust aid in recognizing seriously suicidal persons, lending itself to use by clinical assistants without extensive training who may screen large numbers of patients with its aid.

Neurochemical examination of cerebrospinal fluid has opened another avenue in recognizing suicidal patients. Some ten years ago reports began to appear in the literature that the concentration of 5-hydroxyindoleacetic acid (5-HIAA), a metabolite of serotonin, was unusually low in suicidal patients' spinal fluid, but not in that of patients who were non-suicidally depressed (Asberg 1976). The specific lowering of 5-HIAA has also been reported in suicidal patients who bear other than diagnoses of depression—personality disorder, anxiety state, schizophrenia. It is plausible to assume that the lowering of this substance reflects a decrease in the turnover of serotonin in the brain. Inhibition of serotonin synthesis can provoke aggression in animals, and serotonin sensitive neurons probably are involved in the control of aggression (Lidberg 1984; Brown 1982; Meyerson 1982).

Traskman and his colleagues studied thirty patients who had attempted suicide, comparing them with forty-five healthy volunteers (1981). As expected the suicide attempters, especially those who had made more violent attempts, had lower spinal fluid 5-HIAA levels than the volunteers. A follow-up study of these and another eighty-nine patients who were depressed and/or suicidal disclosed that 20 percent of those whose 5-HIAA levels were below the median were dead within a year.

Whether this test will ever be applied widely as a clinical aid in estimating suicide danger remains to be seen. If research shows that there is a close correlation between depressed spinal fluid 5-HIAA levels and a high score on Beck's hopelessness scale, perhaps it will not, since administering a paper-and-pencil test is less distressing to all than lumbar puncture. Some patients have received Rorschach and spinal fluid examinations at the same time; those with lowered 5-HIAA levels showed higher hostility and anxiety responses in the Rorschach ratings. Their anxiety tolerance was lower, and they managed conflict poorly (Rydin 1982). At the present, neurochemical measures of suicide danger remain in the domain of clinical investigation.

Statistical and diagnostic approaches to recognizing suicidal patients are helpful, but used alone they lead to results that are too ambiguous, showing us no more than which patients are probably at substantial risk. The same is the case with psychological testing. The usefulness of biochemical measures is still under investigation. Yet the clinician, confronted with an individual patient, must decide whether suicide is likely now; on his decision depends not only necessary planning for hospital admission or discharge, for example, but quite possibly the patient's life.

The final decisions must rest on individual clinical study, the integration of the patient's history and mental status examination with what we know about psychodynamic vulnerability to suicide. This we call the psychodynamic formulation of the case.

4.

The Formulation of Suicide Risk

The assessment of suicide risk is a common and often urgent task for clinicians in the emergency departments of general hospitals, psychiatric outpatient clinics, and their consulting rooms. Many patients will present themselves in a state of crisis; others will be brought by concerned relatives and friends after a suicide threat or an attempt.

Statistically, suicide is especially likely to occur in patients who suffer from major depressive illnesses, schizoaffective disorders, and alcoholism, yet vulnerability to suicide is found at all levels of *descriptive* psychopathology and normalcy. Suicide claims victims in all the different diagnostic categories of standard psychiatric nomenclature—psychotic and neurotic patients may kill themselves, as may those with character disorders. So may addicts, patients with brain diseases, and those who bear no diagnosis at all. Outwardly manifest adaptation does not necessarily betray the structural deficiency that makes a patient reliant on external sustaining resources. So long as the sustaining resource is steadily available there may be no manifest symptoms at all.

Imagine, for instance, a successful surgeon who appears outwardly well balanced and professionally successful. What if he suffers a serious hand injury that puts an end to his career in the operating room? Under any circumstances one might expect a temporary drop in self-esteem, sadness, perhaps a loss of appetite. He would feel at a loss professionally; there would be grieving. But after a term of deep but endurable discouragement, a career reorientation would occur, a renewed interest in life would show itself. Were other symptoms to develop, such as indigestion or chronic abdominal pain, a diagnosis of depression with a hypochondriacal psychophysiological reaction might be made. Were delusions, a thought disorder, or hallucinations to appear, the surgeon might qualify for a diagnosis of one of the psychoses. Perhaps he might move in an alcoholic direction. Were it the case that his professional success had been essential as an exterior sustaining resource to regulate self-esteem and protect from primaeval affects, however, he might be flooded by stark fears, murderous rage, violent self-derision; he might begin to daydream about suicide. Despairing, he could do away with himself.

A careful psychiatric history and mental status examination will yield the information necessary to assess the patient's dependency on exterior sustaining resources. The integration of the history and observations of the patient results in the formulation of his vulnerability to suicide. We use the data of the history and mental status examination to identify the patient's idiosyncratic personality vulnerabilities, to assess the degree to which particular psychological injuries of specific types activate his vulnerabilities, and to anticipate characteristic reactions to these injuries.

The examiner begins by learning all he can about the circumstances that surround the present crisis. It is important that the patient be provided with quiet surroundings, and that the examiner convey his wish to help and understand without an attitude of hurry.

These preliminary points seem obvious in themselves, but they deserve to be stressed. Overworked hospital residents laboring in rushed hospital emergency rooms should remember that if a quiet, unhurried setting for the interview is provided, much more can be learned, and more rapidly. (This point escapes too many hospital administrators responsible for the physical settings of such places.) With practice one can gather enough data in the space of an hour to arrive at an intelligent formulation. Rushing matters or offending the patient with unempathic, rapid quizzing only provokes concealing and withholding.

Wherever possible relatives and friends should be interviewed; when he is in an emotionally overwrought condition, the patient's capacity to give a full description of his predicament is often compromised. A few words with someone familiar usually produces important information that otherwise would be overlooked or concealed.

The psychodynamic formulation of suicide risk is rooted in the clinical history. The history of the present illness will help identify what sustaining resources in the present have failed and how the patient is responding to their loss. The mental state examination allows assessment of the current subjective distress, and, coupled with the history of the present illness, can reveal to what degree the patient is slipping into an ego regression. The past history will show not only the patient's past reliance on sustaining resources, but also what symptoms he typically develops when deprived of them. Psychodynamic formulation organizes the history; it aims to show how the patient is reliant on sustaining resources, what is happening to him now that they are disturbed, what disposed him to be reliant on them, and what his characteristic response is likely to be when faced with such a misfortune.

This approach is useful not only in the emergency setting, but also during subsequent management and psychotherapy. Formulation enables us to specify the particular kind of stress to which the patient at hand is uniquely intolerant. Knowing what kind of sustaining resource the patient must have and how he is likely to respond when the resource is threatened, those responsible for his care will know what to watch for, and can be forearmed.

The Circumstances of the Present Crisis

First of all the patient must be given ample opportunity to state his own case; he will need to say just how he feels, and should be encouraged to explain what in his life he cannot bear. Determine what has happened to make the patient feel so overwhelmed, when the trouble began, what interference in functioning has resulted, what the patient is experiencing subjectively, and what impetus to suicide there may be.

Find out whom the patient has told about the suicide he thinks he may commit. Of course, many people threaten to kill themselves without ever intending really to do so, but those who do commit suicide usually let someone else know about it in advance. Those told are emotionally important to the patient. Every disclosure of suicidal ideas should be taken seriously and investigated. Examiners will need to decide whether a suicidal communication is a clear statement of suicidal intent, an emotionally desperate plea for help, or a threat of social blackmail intended to force compliance from someone else (Murphy 1968).

Notice the patient's age, sex, marital status, living arrangements, and physical health. In beginning the history, orient yourself in a general way to the patient's overall statistical risk, recalling that the elderly (especially white males over the age of fifty), the recently separated and divorced, the socially isolated, and patients with histories of major depression, alcoholism, serious previous attempts, and physical illness are at special hazard.

If an actual attempt at self-harm has occurred, what did the patient intend? Not every self-mutilation has personal death as its goal. On the other hand superficial self-injuries that seem of minor consequence, such as pricking oneself with a pin, sometimes conceal intense and dangerous impulses to self-destruction.

Try to classify an attempt according to its lethality. Some patients really intend to die; others, more ambivalent, are gamblers, and leave survival to chance. A third group, strictly speaking not suicidal attempters at all, fully expect to be saved (Farberow 1961). Bear in mind, however, that though today's gesture may not be lethally intended, it warns of possible suicide danger in the future.

The gravity of an attempt can be assessed by weighing three aspects: the patient's intention, the nature of what he has done, and the social context in which he has carried it out.

Correct assessment of intention is difficult; because powerful unconscious factors shape every attempt, the patient may not be fully aware of what he aims to accomplish. Some, fully bent on self-destruction, so far as they are aware, unwittingly arrange a setting so that rescue takes place. Others, intending no more than a gesture, swallow more pills than planned. Were it otherwise, we might take every patient's word for it, and believe him completely when he announces unhesitatingly that he intends to live or to die.

Understanding the patient's intention requires that we investigate his awareness of the effect of his behavior on others, his grasp of what his behavior would mean in terms of his own life, his appreciation of the real consequences of the method employed, and what plans for being rescued, or gambling with a rescue, he made before harming himself. Look for clues of unconscious forces at work in what he arranged. Is there evidence that he unconsciously warned others of what he intended, so that unwittingly he arranged to be saved?

The attempt should be examined in terms of the patient's manifest communication—just what messages, verbal and nonverbal, did he send? It is in fact unusual for a person to give no indications of suicidal decision; the failure to do so suggests a high lethal intent. Clues are commonly given in the form of subtle, indirect allusions, but sometimes the patient will directly tell someone what he intends to do.

What did the patient *intend* to communicate? A desolate remark about committing suicide may be a plea for help in which the patient wants to be comforted and does not really mean to carry through. If unheeded he may carry out a suicidal act that makes the same plea, more actively this time, exerting more force on others. At other times a suicidal announcement amounts to no more than a flat statement of the intent to die, and the patient will not consciously wish to have anyone intervene.

To whom was the pre-attempt communication addressed? Did he let someone know who might reasonably be expected to react with a life-saving intervention? That would make the attempt less dangerous. Did he warn someone predictably indifferent, or even hostile? The chances for a helping response would then be less, and the attempt more dangerous.

Finally, examine the attempt in terms of what the patient has done to himself. It is possible to rank the various methods of suicide in descending order of hazard: using firearms and explosives is probably the most dangerous, followed by jumping from high places, cutting and piercing vital organs, hanging, jumping into deep water when one cannot swim, ingesting poisonous substances, cutting and piercing nonvital organs, jumping into deep water when one can swim, inhaling gas, and ingesting analgesics and sedatives (Tabachnick 1961; Beck 1975a).

Having obtained some understanding of the lethality of the attempt, or in the absence of an attempt, of what the patient may have told others about the attempt he is planning, investigate next what stress has precipitated the current crisis. Systematically look for difficulty with *exterior sustaining resources.*

The chances are excellent some important person has proven a disappointment. Quite probably the patient has been thrown into disequilibrium because of the withdrawal, real or apparent, of someone who has been essential for keeping his balance. The discouraged patient, reluctant to tell a strange examiner everything about a very painful recent emotional wound, may try to conceal a serious fresh loss, or to gloss it over, declaring there has been nothing worth living for in years. After all, recalling the details of an ungrieved loss hurts.

Should you learn that the patient has indeed been disappointed, left, or otherwise deprived of someone important to him, decide whether the critical other person has in fact become unavailable or only seems unavailable to the patient. The friend on whom one has relied may remain a friend, but seem false, because of some imagined slight or injury. In such a case the danger may pass when the patient's false perception is corrected.

In the event the sustaining friend is in fact unavailable, it will be necessary to decide whether the loss is a permanent or a temporary one. The friend away on vacation but due home on a known date is different from the friend who is dying of a terminal disease or who has become disgusted with the patient's anxious demands and has permanently withdrawn.

Are there other people available to the patient to meet the need for sustaining? If so, where are they, and how quickly and how unambivalently are they likely to respond? If there are others available, will they be acceptable to the patient? One must bear in mind that not all patients are prepared to accept substitute sustainers, even if they are available, and that many are incapable of doing so when they feel acutely bereft. It is important to find out how welcome such substitutes may be. The patient in the following case could not easily use others as sustaining resources.

Case 20. Mr. Y. was a solitary 27-year-old former graduate student with a history of many very serious suicide attempts, even though he was surrounded by a caring family who made available to him the best of psychiatric treatment. He had rejected a number of competent therapists, and showed little interest in other people. He had been unable to continue with treasured career plans after developing a schizophrenic illness, and was much invested in autistic daydreams, some of which had to do with the bliss he imagined he might experience in the afterlife.

When patients are particularly fastidious about grasping the sustaining hands that others reach out, or when no such hands are offered, hospital admission may well be in order. Over a period of time, with sensitive handling, it is sometimes possible for such patients to accept a sustaining relationship from someone in a formal psychotherapeutic capacity.

In reviewing the patient's human resources or lack thereof, do not overlook the possibility that someone may actively want him dead. From time to time one encounters a situation in which a spouse or a parent may say, in effect, "Why don't you go ahead and kill yourself and be done with it? You're no good to yourself or to anybody else, and besides, you're making me sick with all your suicide talk!"

More commonly lethal wishes from important others will be covert, expressed, perhaps, by silent withdrawal or emotional frigidity. Patients may make suicide threats and be ignored; they may bring to someone else's attention that a dangerous drug overdose has been ingested, only to be met with indifferent inaction. Sometimes lethal wishes are concealed behind attitudes of saccharine solicitude. A spouse or parent may repeatedly enquire, "Are you thinking about taking pills again, dear? I am so worried about you!" This kind of fretful care may destroy the patient's tenuous self-confidence, heighten dependency, encourage primitive regression, and promote suicide.

No small number of patients in suicidal crises are engaged in some form of psychotherapy. Inasmuch as the therapist is often the patient's only sustaining resource, one could predict that suicide ought to take place at times when the therapist is not available. Of course this is the case. Vacations are times of danger. Sometimes the patient may feel that the therapist is about to throw him out of the treatment; indeed, sometimes intimations in that direction will have been made. Whenever possible it is important to discuss the state of the patient's treatment with the therapist; transference-countertransference impasses lie behind many suicidal crises.

The identification of such an impasse may be life-saving for the patient, but its correct handling is difficult. Because everyone concerned in these situations tends to blame somebody for the boggle, the therapist may feel threatened, guilty, and defensive. Not every therapist has been successfully trained in the management of suicidal patients and the countertransference responses they evoke. Having become embroiled in a frightening situation, he may be preparing to take flight. Consultation with an expert in these circumstances can save the patient and sometimes improve therapeutic skills (Maltsberger 1984).

Most patients rely on other people for sustaining friendships, but remember there may be other companions as well. Has the patient lost a pet? The reader may recall Mr. G. (Case 19), whose suicide attempt with digitalis superficially appeared to be a "rational" one, an effort by a sick old man to end a life of meaningless suffering. What in fact made life meaningless for Mr. G. was the loss of his dog Fidel, not his physical ills. Sometimes patients of this sort will accept the substitution of a new pet more readily than another person for a sustaining resource. Pets may seem less treacherous and more dependable; they do not threaten with some of the complexities of human companionship. The painful pressures of sexual and aggressive excitement, sometimes intolerable in a close relationship with someone else, are not such a problem with pets. Furthermore, important fantasies can be elaborated with pets that human friendship may exclude. One suicidal patient had a succession of cats over a lifetime; when one died, she would replace it with another and give it the same name. The patient believed that the soul of her original pet transmigrated again and again into new kittens in order to remain near her.

Sometimes a patient can be thrown into a suicidal crisis because he is convinced some misdeed or another has caused God to turn his back in unforgiving wrath. The Blessed Virgin or a favorite saint, the patient may be convinced, has grown hopelessly disgusted. Ask after the patient's religious life to look for possibilities of this sort. Quite commonly the God or the saint on which the patient depends will bear little resemblance to those of ordinary Church belief; the patient's holy figure may be capricious, malignant, and changeable in the extreme, but seem very real indeed. Patients are sometimes unwilling to disclose these special relationships to unsympathetic examiners; they are afraid they will seem foolish or be taken for mad.

Sometimes we do not understand that a patient is suffering from the loss of a sustaining person because the fractured relationship has been almost entirely a relationship in fantasy. Schizoid people may manage to go along for many years trusting that sooner or later a remote acquaintance, or even a stranger, may make a proposal of marriage or a declaration of friendship, when there is in fact no realistic basis for such an expectation. Should events evolve so that the unrealistic hopes are shattered, the patients can fall prey to despair and the painful affects that accompany it. Neither the person who has proven so bitterly disappointing nor others who know the patient are likely to understand the real nature of the loss.

Bearing in mind that some patients have little interest in others at all but live literally for their work, inquire about career or job difficulties, promotions hoped for but not received, transfers from one department to another, from one city to another. Is the new office manager less supportive than the one who has just retired? In reviewing the importance of work as a sustaining resource, try to separate how much the patient has needed the work itself to keep in balance from how much the patient has needed the supportive admiration and regard of work associates. Often enough one learns that both are important for survival; sometimes outstanding work performance is the coin with which he purchases the respect and admiration of others; the specific appreciation of one or two special as-sociates may be less important than the sense that a large number of comparative strangers admire the patient from a distance. Such patients experience life as though they were starring actors on a stage, bowing to the applause of a large audience whose faces are blurred across the footlights, but whose appreciation is enthusiastic, however anonymous.

Case 21. Prof. R., a prominent engineer in his later sixties, became acutely suicidal when forced to retire because of his age. He had been a lonely child in a large family; the first emotional notice he recalled came in elementary school, where his teachers recognized him as a child of extraordinary talent. Without difficulty he completed university studies at a precociously young age and began a long and distinguished teaching and research career that earned him an inter-national reputation. He was emotionally aloof from others, but relished the recognition and praise his work and talent brought him. The love of his family brought little consolation as he contemplated a retirement which to him was no better than a "living death." Declaring that nothing remained for him in the future except senility and physical decay, he determined to "beat the game" by destroying his body and "escaping" before he was ravaged by old age. He had begun plans to do away with himself, but set these aside when arrangements were made for him to continue teaching and working as a special scholar in his old department.

A sense of personal status may depend on achieving and maintaining a certain financial status; for some it is the proven ability to earn large sums of money on which self-esteem depends. Personal worth can become equated with material worth. The numerous suicides that followed the 1929 stock market collapse illustrate this point. For professional and business people with substantial earning capacities, a sudden change in financial status can provoke a suicidal crisis.

It is rare that work alone, if not rewarded by some degree of recognition from others (even if the recognition is a rather vague, general one, such as a general appreciation from the broader scientific community) is sufficient to sustain a suicide vulnerable person. Thomas Creech (1659-1700), the eminent classical scholar and translator, wrote in the margin of his work on Lucretius, "N.B. I must remember to hang myself when I have finished my commentary," which he did, some twenty years later (Fedden 1938:240). In 1735 John Robeck, the Swedish philosopher, wrote a long, Stoic defense of suicide. When his work was done he gave away all his property and drowned himself (Alvarez 1972). Were these two scholars examples of the rare types who lived solely for their work and were not much concerned with other people, but with the intellectual life only?

In trying to understand what may have precipitated the present crisis, ask about the patient's health; *most* of the patients who commit suicide are physically sick; many have serious illnesses. Dorpat (1960) found that 51 percent of the suicides in his series were seriously medically ill; 80 percent of Koranyi's (1977) series were unwell, and Marshall (1983) reported that cancer patients commit suicide 50 to 100 percent more often than nonpatient controls. From the psychodynamic point of view this is not difficult to understand. Physical illness is very likely to interfere with every class of sustaining resource on which a suicide vulnerable individual may rely. Illness may force old men and women out of familiar homes and neighborhoods into isolated institutions, so that important relationships are disrupted (cf. Case 19). It can interrupt or put an end to valued work. Prized athletic skill or other self-aspects that have sustained patients for years may be destroyed by illness. Surgery can spell the loss of valued bodily functions and disrupt important relationships. In this connection it is important to find out about the patient's sexual life. While this area of experience is not critically important to everyone, some individuals (men especially) seem to judge themselves principally according to a standard of sexual performance. These people cannot feel worthwhile unless they test themselves from time to time and repeatedly prove sexually lively and adequate. They may have regular recourse to prostitutes or strangers in order to check their virility. A graduate student once described his compulsive sexual activity as periodically having to pass a "phallic examination."

Case 6 portrays the lonely life of an actuary and the special relationship he has with his much prized body, kept in splendid trim through regular swimming. Case 7 describes the predicament of the aging restaurateur whose adored penis had failed him. Dorpat (1968) reported a suicidal patient who became impotent after prostate surgery and several women who killed themselves after hysterectomies.

Patients can be asked, "What in the past has given you any interest to keep on living?" in an effort to learn about special personal investments of this sort. Bear in mind that not only muscular or sexual functions may be prized as special "friends" in this sense, but intellectual ones as well. Imagine a solitary eccentric whose sole consolation lies in an extraordinary talent for solving crossword puzzles. When he is almost overwhelmed with self-reproach and solitude, working out a particularly difficult puzzle might bring enough self-content to make life endurable. The development of a mild memory-loss in later life could threaten such a person's survival.

While looking carefully for disturbances in exterior sustaining resources—relationships with others (including pets and heavenly companions), work disturbances, loss of prized self-functions—it is helpful to pay attention to the timing of symptom development. The loss most closely followed in time by the appearance of symptoms will likely be more significant to the patient's developing illness than another of an earlier date.

What *interference with function* is developing in the course of the crisis? Are there signs that the patient's investment in the world around him is seriously diminished? After a loss most people temporarily lose some of their interest in others and in activities ordinarily highly valued; Freud (1917) described this as a withdrawal of libido from the object world. Healthier patients, however, do not withdraw so profoundly as do those who are suicide prone. Look out for indications that ties to others, to work, and to hitherto interesting parts of oneself are being cast permanently aside.

Is the patient refusing to have anything to do with former friends and associates? Has he grown paranoid and suspicious, accusing everyone of falseness? Is there a change in his capacity for work? If he is not able to work as well as ordinarily, is this a matter of concern to him, or does he treat it with indifference? When a former serious, hard worker shrugs off a new work incapacity, he may be close to despair. Indifference to previously important work may indicate abandonment of a once valued sustaining resource.

Frequently one will detect a dangerous "domino effect"; the patient, having suffered an important blow, responds by further withdrawal from secondary resources of support that he can ill afford to lose. A vulnerable man whose wife leaves him may refuse to see his family or friends; he may stop going to work. In this way his difficulty can be compounded. Take care to identify what the primary loss has been; secondary losses brought about by the patient's reaction to the primary one may not be so much the critical causes of the present illness as they are its consequences.

Try to understand to what degree the patient has brought about the critical disappointment, and to what degree it has happened because of circumstances beyond his control. If the patient has provoked the critical disappointment, as is often enough the case, an important point for future treatment will have been uncovered. Some patients are quite oblivious to the fact that they repeatedly provoke the rejections they so much fear; anticipating abandonment, they may behave in clinging, demanding, and reproachful ways toward others, inviting re-peated rejection and disappointment.

In weighing the degree to which functioning is impaired, pay particular attention to the abandonment of important object ties. The patient who begins to destroy prized souvenirs or possessions, to make a will, and to avoid old friends and associations may be giving up on life.

Case 22. Mary N., a 29-year-old woman with a borderline personality disorder, had been admitted to the hospital with a major depression. After Miss N. suffered a minor disappointment with her therapist, a nurse discovered her systematically defacing and destroying photo-graphs of her friends and her family, the contents of an album which previously had given her much pleasure. Tactful enquiry revealed that she had made up her mind that morning to kill herself; before that time, she had been ambivalent about suicide.

With the arrival and intensification of the primitive affects associated with suicide, at a time when he is deprived of the resources on which he would ordinarily rely, the patient may have recourse to *regressive measures for self-comforting* that are not consistent with self-respect and are not typical of his ordinary adaptive style. Look for evidence that the patient is being driven to these measures, bearing in mind that because they are often experienced as shameful he may find their acknowledgement painful, and expecting to be condemned, conceal them.

Some patients begin to drink heavily, relying on alcohol to soften the bite of conscience. Many years ago an aging professor of archaeology, his brilliant career seriously compromised because of the alcohol he used to make solitude endurable, hoarsely whispered to me: "Vitamin W., boy, vitamin W. They didn't teach you about that one in medical school, but it's the most important of them all. Whiskey! It takes the edge off a cruel world."

The pharmacology of alcohol is such that while anxiety and guilt relief may be experienced in states of mild intoxication, disintoxication is marked by worsening of depression. Patients are likely to say or to do things while in a state of alcoholic disinhibition that can be sources of great guilt and shame when sobriety returns. About a fourth of the patients who commit suicide are in fact alcoholics; the risk increases as chronicity lengthens. A startling proportion of successful suicides take place under the immediate influence of alcohol, even though the diagnostic criteria for chronic alcoholism may not be fully satisfied. Remember, too, that alcoholics in particular are loss sensitive. Upwards of a third of the alcoholics who die by their own hands have recently lost an important sustaining relationship. (Robins 1981, 1959; Murphy 1979, 1967). Alcohol promotes the decay of already weakened reality-testing capacities and loosens impulse control. A patient in a suicidal crisis, drinking to relieve subjective distress, can in fact bring himself perilously close to suicidal action without recognizing what he is doing. Some, hesitating to go forward, may drink on purpose in order to disinhibit themselves and cloud consciousness enough to make suicidal action easier.

The clouding of consciousness that results from alcohol use may in itself dispose to suicidal action, quite apart from the disinhibiting effect unhappily familiar in any busy emergency room. When a patient is unable to think clearly and burdened with painful affects, intoxication probably makes it more difficult for him to remember better alternatives than suicide by interfering with the capacity for creative fantasy (Corey 1977). Drugs are another regressive, comforting resource. Cocaine, now a serious public health problem, is well known for its euphoric properties and, like alcohol, may temporarily relieve depression but worsen it in the long run. Sedatives of various kinds are available in the streets. Barbiturates are now more difficult to obtain and more dangerous than the benzodiazepene compounds which have replaced them. But the benzodiazepenes, too, while giving some temporary solace, will leave the patient with a habit if they are not carefully managed and worse off in the long run.

Suicide prone patients are likely to become addicted to all such substances, and it is easier to act suicidally when under the influence of any of the sedatives. Although some have tended to blame barbiturate deaths on "drug automatism" (the patient, sedated, is thought to have forgotten taking a previous dose, and so repeats it, unwittingly overdosing), in fact most overdoses are probably motivated by the wish to escape from pain and possibly to sleep forever (Dorpat 1974).

After years of faithful monogamy, heterosexual patients may, in a suicidal crisis, find themselves behaving promiscuously; some will start to seek out homosexual encounters, looking for reassurance and escape from the unendurable distress of suicidal affects. When such behavior is inconsistent with the patient's self-respect, one may expect a worsening of depressive difficulties. Already self-contemptuous, the patient now becomes self-disgusted as well.

Still others may begin to gamble in an attempt at self-distraction, perhaps losing money and making a bad situation worse.

Young Adults

Although the examination of young people who are at risk for suicide should follow the same general outline employed for adults, there are some special points that require notice. Suicide is quite a rare phenomenon in young children, but the incidence increases very rapidly with the appearance of adolescence.

Adolescents differ from adults in that the mental structures necessary to avoid excessive dependence on sustaining resources outside the patient's self are still in the process of development. All adolescents may be assumed to be substantially reliant on such sustaining resources, just as young children are. In most instances (but by no means all) a young person will require the love, praise, and comfort of his parents from time to time. Most adolescents have not yet built up for themselves sufficient work capacity and experience for work itself to serve a sustaining function, although some students from an early age are intensely invested in excelling academically. For these, academic failure can represent a severe narcissistic injury and precipitate a suicidal crisis.

Suicide threats from children and adolescents must always be taken seriously and investigated; examiners should not be reluctant to ask directly about suicidal ideation, impulses, and planning.

Suicide in children and adolescents very commonly takes place in the context of family disruption; alcoholism, quarreling, open threats of abandonment, and sometimes suicidal threatening trouble these families. Be alert for the fact that conflicts are sometimes enacted around a child who has been selected by the family to play the scapegoat. Scapegoating and blaming of this kind, the expression of homicidal wishes in many cases, should be watched for—they can provoke suicide (Sabbath 1969).

Suggestion probably operates more forcibly in the adolescent group than among adults. Adolescents tend to share a group ideal; their personal self ideals (ego ideals) are still developing. Suicide epidemics affecting specific school populations or geographic areas have been reported recently in the public press. Adolescent suicide is not, however, primarily an impulsive act, even though it sometimes appears to be so. On the contrary, it is commonly the end point of a pathological ego regression that has been going on for some time, and which may be recognized by an examiner on the alert. The suggestion that an adolescent suicide epidemic affords and the impulsivity that characterizes some adolescents, may set an attempt into motion among those who are psychologically ready.

A number of adolescents who have made dangerous suicide attempts have been studied psychodynamically by a group in London. Novick (1984) published the results of this investigation, describing a series of developments called the "suicide sequence"; recognition of such a sequence unfolding is a clear indication of serious danger. The sequence is this:

Typical suicidal adolescents will have felt depressed and sexually abnormal for some time, and they will have been suicidally preoccupied as well. They will not have achieved satisfactory separation from their mothers; in fact, it is quite usual that both boys and girls will be locked into an intense sadomasochistic attachment to the mother from which escape is impossible. The sequence leading to attempted suicide is set into motion when external events demand a step that threatens to break the tie to the mother. Quite often this will be high school graduation, taking a first job, or going away to college.

The adolescent fails to make the necessary step; the demand the external world seems to make and the failure to meet it lead to a worsening of emotional distress, and the adolescent becomes acutely aware of his dependency on the mother. The failure to make the normal adolescent move away from her leads to an intensification of a longstanding sadomasochistic entanglement. A girl, terrified of being abandoned by her mother, unconsciously hating her, and longing to be free, may submit to her while at the same time repeatedly creating situations which drive the mother away.

All sexual and aggressive preoccupations, which are often quite intense, become a source of increasing anxiety in the context of a heightened awareness of dependency. Some adolescents will develop a shadowy awareness that their fantasies are incestuous. In order to escape from a very dangerous situation, with murderous and incestuous impulses threatening to break through into awareness, the adolescent will appeal to somebody else to rescue him.

Quite commonly this comes in the form of a suicide threat. If there is a helpful response the lethal sequence may be interrupted; professional help may become available. If not, murderous feelings toward the mother will soon break through to awareness, and these will be accompanied by intense guilt. The suicide thoughts which have been present for some time will now take on a new importance—suicide seems the only possible resolution. Suicide may even seem heroic. Totally preoccupied with suicidal impulses, the adolescent will now turn again to the outside world, but this time not for help. Unconsciously the patient provokes a rejection from someone not the mother. Suicide can then occur with attention centered on someone else; mother is not seen as the person to blame. By provoking rejection from someone else, he can avoid conscious awareness that the suicide is an aggressive attack on the mother.

The patient hopes suicide will produce a number of results: reassertion of control over exterior events, over others, and over his own body. There are commonly revenge fantasies;

conceiving himself to be the victim of others, he imagines they will be sorry for what they have done to him.

It is well to bear in mind that behind a suicidal adolescent there may be a suicidal adult (Margolin 1968). Many mothers of such adolescents are themselves suicidally preoccupied, and some of them actively try to bring about their own deaths by provoking their children to kill them. Such a mother may say, "Go ahead! Kill me! You don't care about me anyway! Get it over with!"

Having gathered the available information about the nature of the present crisis, the examiner can now work out for himself the degree to which the patient has been deprived of the resources on which he ordinarily relies to maintain a sense of personal well-being. He can see just what the critical sustaining resources have been, what symptoms the patient has developed as a consequence of their loss, to what degree the patient's symptoms compound the difficulty by inviting secondary losses, whether the patient is abandoning interest in customary areas of emotional investment, and to what degree he is having recourse to unusual, dangerous, or self-esteem damaging measures to relieve himself.

Still to be discussed is the assessment of the patient's subjective state of mind. While many inferences can be drawn about the patient's emotional and mental experience during the course of history taking, further specific inquiry is in order once the history of the present illness has been collected.

The Mental State Examination

Discussion of the mental state examination must begin with a warning. Of course mental state observations are indispensable, but there is a wide-spread tendency to place almost exclusive reliance on the patient's *manifest mood* in deciding whether or not he is at suicide risk. While manifest mood is important to notice, it is a poor indicator of suicide readiness. Indeed, many patients cheer up when at last they decide to die. Neither is it wise to believe a patient who denies any suicidal intent when there is evidence from the history that he is suicide vulnerable and reliant for sustenance on exterior resources that have plainly failed him.

In the course of taking the patient's history the examiner will have noticed many details concerning the patient's *general appearance and behavior.* A close survey of such details will give many clues to the degree of the patient's anxiety, his self-regard, how difficult it may be for him to control himself, how hopeless he may feel, and whether psychosis may be a factor. Apart from taking note of the patient's general bearing and demeanor, the examiner will want to notice how the patient stands or sits. Are there oddities or mannerisms? Does he seem tense, panicky, withdrawn, suspicious? Peering obliquely from the corners of the eyes and wearing dark glasses indoors are typical paranoid behavior. Does the patient seem disheveled, careless about his clothing? Physical neglect can indicate self-contempt just as it may signal dementia. The face may be contorted with fury; it may be white with terror. Anguished facial expressions, plucking at the clothes of passers-by, and hand-wringing are all typical of patients in agitated states of depression who are suffering the terrible affects of melancholia. A haughty, grandiose air is suggestive not only of paranoid trends, but also of narcissistic brittleness; the patient who needs to deprecate others is often attempting to aggrandize himself at their expense.

A past history of self-mutilation may be inferred from multiple scars on the forearms; a tracheostomy scar in the jugular notch between the clavicles suggests a patient who has recovered from a self-induced coma from overdosing. Scars and needle marks noticed during the course of the physical examination can give similar clues about addiction and old self-injury.

From the beginning of the initial interview the examiner will be concerned with the patient's subjective state, or *mood.* Alert to the possibility that the patient may suffer from one or more of the affects that invite suicide, the examiner inquires specifically about each one.

To what extent is the patient suffering from aloneness, in contrast to loneliness—that barren condition that can grow into panic, wherein one feels hopelessly separated from any human relatedness and disintegration is threatened? Patients vulnerable to states of aloneness may have difficulty in describing what they feel; but they often will recognize the difference from loneliness, readily acknowledging that aloneness is the better name. Depersonalization experiences are often associated with this condition; others may seem unreal, and so may one's body. Patients threatened with heightening feelings of aloneness may only with difficulty restrain themselves from running howling through the streets; sometimes they travel from city to city in restless distress hoping to get away from the feeling.

To what extent is the patient self-contemptuous? The examiner should try to discover the degree to which the patient is self-critical. Some may be only mildly so; others may be so self-angry that sitting still may be difficult. Melancholiac guilt can be so intense that the patient paces up and down, crying out for relief, begging to be put to death. He wants not only to escape his agony; convinced of his profound badness, he sees death as the only proper punishment.

Remain on the alert for the patient who expresses a fear of death. One might reason (incorrectly) that the patient who is afraid to die would hardly be likely to destroy himself, but the opposite is the case. Those patients whose unconscious self-murderous impulses are gathering force may develop a morbid fear that death is coming. They sense its approach and dread its inevitable attack.

Case 23. Anna Z., a 23-year-old unmarried clerk admitted to a psychiatric hospital for an acute schizophrenic episode, repeatedly told staff that she was afraid she was about to die, and begged for reassurance that this was not the case. She had not seemed to be suicidal, although she was emotionally quite distressed. Without warning she took a dangerous overdose of pills; for some days it seemed unlikely she would survive.

Many suicidal patients have some subjective sense of inner splitting in the experience of self-contempt. The patient in Case 13, who felt herself trapped with a malignant robot in control of her head, was both victim and executioner. Many patients experience the subjective sense of inner division without actually developing delusions; indeed, the pitiful woman possessed by the robot was speaking metaphorically. When the sense of division is extreme and depersonalization enters the picture, a psychosis may lie over the horizon.

The patient trapped with the robot inside her head had the subjective experience of feeling detached from herself and watching herself, as it were, from outside. Some patients describe encountering images of themselves when awake, either in hallucinatory experiences or in vivid fantasies and illusions. Schilder (1950) described the process whereby some patients double their body-images and project them into the external world; he called it "autoscopy." Freud (1919) believed that a double might appear as the consequence of dissociation of the superego from the ego, making it possible for the patient to treat himself as an object.

To the double can be attributed all the wishes and strivings which have been repudiated under the demands of development and repressed. Projection onto the double may make it seem fearsome and foreign to the self; it threatens to put into action the very impulses which with great emotional expense the patient has disavowed and driven out of awareness into the unconscious. Ostow (1960) reported the case of a young man whose double came into the room where he sat reading, went to the medicine closet, and took an overdose of sleeping pills.

Poe (1839) described the life-long harrassment of one William Wilson, a fictional character beset by a double who bears the same name, was born on the same day, and who persecutes him through school and adult years by dressing in the same way, whispering his very words in sardonic echo, and mocking at him in the way a hallucinatory persecutor might do. When at last poor Wilson attacks his double, he realizes that he has attacked and fatally injured his own image in a mirror, and that in doing so, he has killed himself psychically. Autoscopic experiences (described in detail by Lukianowicz [1958]) should alert the examiner to suicidal danger. Suicide is sometimes preceded by autoscopic dreams of accidents and death.

In assessing the quality of fury that afflicts suicidal patients it is important to distinguish between rage of ordinary proportions and rage of murderous proportions. Ask the patient what his anger is like, how he feels it, whether it is homicidal in tone. Polite elderly ladies and gentlemen, whose manners would seem to preclude such passion may harbor it nevertheless, and it is a mistake not to ask.

Who and what seems to be the target of the patient's hostility? Is it directed at someone else, at an institution or an organization, at the patient's self, or at some portion of the patient's body? Does the patient's body feel as though it is his own, a part of himself, or does it seem to be alien, possibly somebody else's? If this is the case, obviously reality-testing and self-object differentiation are weakening and the danger may be substantial. If the patient is murderously angry at somebody else, is he comfortable with it, or is he outraged with himself and feeling that punishment is in order? In the former case homicide may be a danger; in the latter, suicide.

Enquire about the affect states that lead directly to suicide, but find out also whether the patient feels enough self-regard to care about saving himself. Some patients are so limited in self-regard that their survival is a matter of indifference. Does the patient attach any importance to whether or not he is uncomfortable, cold, thirsty, hungry, in need of medical attention? People who are unable to care about themselves, their physical and emotional needs, are often limited in their ability to resist suicidal pressures. They don't seem worth saving to themselves.

How depressed is the patient? Does he feel low in mood, has he lost interest in his usual pursuits? The examiner will ask about insomnia or excessive sleeping, loss of energy, decreased effectiveness or productivity at school, work or home. Is the patient suffering from difficulty in paying attention? Is concentration difficult? Are there spells of crying?

More important than depression is the degree to which the patient has given way to despair. Repeated studies show that it is the patient's hopelessness which predisposes to suicide more than lowered spirits or retardation (Beck 1975a; Kovacs 1975; Dorpat 1967; Wetzel 1976). That is why it is critically important to ask the patient if he has given up hope for his life. The general question should be followed by more limited and specific questions: has the patient given up hope that he may one day feel happier, does he believe that his relationships with others can improve? Does he believe that others will ever again care about him and what he feels and needs? Above all, the examiner will want to learn whether the patient has decided that it is useless to hope any more. The situation is dangerous if the patient has given up, deciding not to try and not to want anything or anyone again.

While a depressed, discouraged mood may be a danger signal, many patients commit suicide while not visibly depressed. Indeed, in some instances, as Case 24 below will illustrate, depression lifts when the patient makes up his mind to put an end to life. Suicides can take place in many moods; it seems probable, however, that most of them occur in despair. Yet giving up on oneself at last can be a relief. The patient who decides to abandon his wretched life may feel his spirits lift, especially if he trusts something better is waiting for him on the other side of the grave.

Examination of the patient's *mental content* will yield information about current preoccupations and reveal disorders of perception and cognition—hallucinations, delusions, and formal disorders of thought.

Obviously, it is important to know to what degree the patient is preoccupied with suicide per se. There are essentially three levels of conscious suicidal preoccupation: fantasy, impulse, and action. At the level of fantasy one may find rare, occasional, or frequent ideas of committing suicide. Sometimes patients are quite attached to such daydreams and find them comforting. There are those who comfort themselves with the thought that if things get very much worse, there is always suicide. The comfort that suicide daydreaming affords should be separated, however, from impulses to commit suicide. To experience a suicidal impulse is to feel a definite push to do away with oneself—it is a definite wish accompanied by an emotional thrust toward action. The third level is action—a physical movement in the direction of carrying out the impulse.

Over the course of a lifetime most people will have, at one time or another, a suicidal fantasy. A life-long preoccupation with committing suicide is, however, another matter; it suggests the presence of an important unconscious complex that includes one or more of the various death fantasies we will take up shortly.

Find out about suicide fantasies in detail. The patient who has a vague idea that he may at some time "end it all" is obviously different from the person who has worked out an imaginary plan. Has the patient chosen the means? What does he imagine the experience of suicide would be like, physically and emotionally? What, if anything, does he believe his suicide would do to others? Has he set a date? Some patients, years in advance, select the birthday after which they will act. Is the suicide plan contingent on some anticipated misfortune in the future, such as the development of a physical illness, or the loss of an important relationship? How lethal are the means the patient plans to employ?

As we have seen earlier, the patient who plans to jump from a high building or shoot himself may seem to be in greater danger than another who is planning to take an overdose of tranquilizer. While the immediate danger may in fact be greater for jumpers or shooters, bear in mind that the overdoser, laboring under the mistaken belief that a handful of pills will be lethal, can be equally intent on ending his life. The gravity of the suicide intent is determined by what the patient believes the consequences of his act will be, not by the factual danger. Sophisticated emergency room physicians, knowing full well that opening a few superficial veins in the wrist will not result in death, are likely to dismiss such cutting as no more than a "gesture"; a naive young woman without anatomical training may think otherwise. Her wrist cutting can express an intent no less lethal than an effort at self-hanging.

Some patients may nurse suicidal fantasies for years without having suicidal impulses. Until impulses appear, suicide is not a danger, but suicidal daydreams cherished over a lifetime can warn that intense suicidal impulses may erupt with little warning. Suicidal impulses can come on suddenly in those who have not been suicide daydreamers as well.

In assessing preparedness for action, it is helpful to know how continuously the patient is preoccupied with suicide and how often he is troubled by impulses to act. Sometimes the impulse to suicidal action is mild and occasional, sometimes it is strong and persisting. It may be intermittent, but intense. The impulse may be almost continuous; resisting it can be exhausting. Quite often one can find out what relieves the patient from the urge to commit suicide by asking; he will commonly know, too, what exacerbates it. The patient's own sense of how well he is resisting suicidal impulses, how long he can hold out, and what he needs to fortify him in the struggle is important to understand.

Though the death-fantasies that are so important in precipitating suicide commonly remain unconscious, they are often not deeply repressed and can fairly readily be elicited. Where the significant fantasy remains unconscious, one may find a patient quite taken with the idea that he will in dying "become" nothing. We have already discussed the universal equation of sleep and death, a metaphor so deeply imbedded in the language, religion and mythology of modern and ancient times that few recognize it as such; it makes suicide in the quest of mindless repose seem comfortably plausible.

The following ideas about death and dying should be looked for:

1. Suicide is a gateway leading into a dreamless sleep (nothingness);
2. It will effect reunion with someone or something which has been lost;
3. It will be a way of escaping from a persecutory enemy, interior or exterior;
4. It will destroy an enemy who seems to have taken up a place in the patient's body or some other part of himself;
5. It will provide a passage into another, better world;
6. One can get revenge on someone else by abandoning him or by destroying his favorite possession (the patient's body), and one can then watch him suffer from beyond the grave.

The fantasy that death is a means of escape from some intolerable present or anticipated future situation is fairly common in patients who are physically unwell. Some of these will take the view that their bodies are little more than physical cages from which suicide promises liberation into some vaguely conceived future state. The aging professor of Case 21 planned to "beat the game" by committing suicide before old age and disease "got him." He personalized disease and physical decay as his enemies and imagined he could escape from his body as though it were a prison. The same thing was eloquently developed by Seneca in his *Epistles;* we find him writing,

. . . if old age begins to shatter my mind, and to pull its various faculties to pieces, if it leaves me, not life, but only the breath of life, I shall rush out of a house that is crumbling and tottering. . . . Live if you so desire; if not, you may return to the place whence you came. . . . a lancet will open the way to that great freedom, and tranquility can be purchased at the cost of a pin-prick.

An explicit believer in the transmigration of souls, Seneca was confident that in death the soul is born again, shedding the body as a newborn infant rids itself of the placenta. The proper domain of the soul, he assured us, is in the vastness of space that encircles the height and breadth of the firmament, where the "sentinel stars take their turn." All time belongs to the soul; among the gods it will find the glow of all the stars as they mingle their fire, and perfected, it will transcend its present darkness and see perfect light. The same fantasy is often entertained in our own times. People committing suicide the day you read this will question no more than Seneca the belief that the mental self can be divided from the physical, that the mental self can survive after death, that old age and disease are personified malicious enemies of the mental self, that the mental self can escape these enemies and run away intact, and that death is a tranquil experience in some better place. Seneca committed suicide in A.D. 65 at the command of the emperor Nero, perhaps not unwillingly.

Form some estimation of the degree to which the patient has lost the capacity to tell whether or not his own body is a part of himself; does he feel at home in it and take it for granted as an integrated self-aspect, or does he experience it as an alien cage in which he is confined, a cage belonging to, or even identified with, someone else? As we have seen previously, some patients mutilate their skins, probably to heighten sensation at the boundary between physical self and the exterior world. They do it to help them feel *contained* in their skins (Novotny 1972). Cutting helps reinforce boundaries between the self and others. Dabrowski (1937) described a small boy who scalded his hand with boiling water, remarking "Only this can bring me back the feeling of myself."

At the same time one must ask whether the patient places a greater emotional value on his fantasies and beliefs concerning suicide and death than he does on reality. Illusions can be cherished with great intensity, especially in circumstances of emotional distress, and, unless they are interfered with, may operate with all the force of delusions.

The actual presence of delusions in depressed patients greatly heightens the likelihood of suicide or serious attempts. Roose and his colleagues have shown that delusionally depressed patients are five times more likely to commit suicide than depressed fellow-sufferers who are delusion-free (1983). This finding is quite consistent with what has been taken for granted in good clinics for years—those depressed patients who are agitated and deluded are at the very highest risk for suicide and need emergency hospital care. Suicidal patients may suffer not only from depressive delusions, but from persecutory ones as well.

The reader may need to be reminded that descriptive psychiatry has long recognized several classes of *depressive delusions.* The patient with *delusions of sin* is convinced he has committed the worst imaginable transgressions, or he magnifies actual minor peccadillos into unpardonable crimes. He expects to be punished in an appalling manner in the present and in the world to come; he may be convinced that he is so wicked that all his relatives, or even the whole world, will also be punished for his evil. *Depressive hypochondriacal delusions* involve the conviction that one is suffering from serious, horrible diseases, though the real disease, melancholia, is denied. Hypochondriacal delusions of this sort differ from the hypochondriacal delusions found in certain paranoid and schizophrenic states without affective disturbance. Depressive hypochondriacal delusions postpone the worst suffering for the future; convinced that his intestines are blocked, the patient with such delusions waits to perish disgustingly and in agony. The paranoid or schizophrenic hypochondriac insists that he is suffering from intestinal inactivity and demands and expects immediate relief. A third form of depressive delusion is that of *impoverishment*; the patient is convinced that he is bankrupt, that he has lost his home and all his possessions, that he and all those whom he loves will have to starve. An unusual form of depressive delusions are those of nihilism, corresponding to the "delire de negation" of French psychiatry. The patient is convinced that everything has ceased to exist—the hospital, the world, God, the other patients. In Cotard's Syndrome, the patient is convinced that he no longer has a body, or that the body that he inhabits, which he recognizes as his own, is already dead. One may find the "delire d'enormité," frequently connected with nihilistic delusions; the patient dares not use the toilet for fear the whole world will be flooded or covered with filth. He is convinced he is swollen with such quantities of excreta that he has expanded to fill the whole house, the whole city. *Megalomanic depressive delusions* occur rarely; such a patient not only believes he is profoundly bad, but may be convinced he is Satan himself or the Antichrist (cf. Case 12).

Persecutory delusions occur not only in paranoid schizophrenic patients, many of whom end their lives in suicide, but in patients with schizoaffective psychoses, other paranoid disorders, and affective psychoses. One should separate *delusions of deserved persecution*, common in psychotic depressions, from the very common *delusions of unjust persecution*, found in schizophrenic disorders. The patient suffering from a delusion of deserved persecution feels that if there is any justice in the world, he will be put to death for his crimes and sins. He may wait fearfully for the arrival of the hangman, but he feels that hanging is what he deserves. Schizophrenic patients suffering from ordinary persecutory delusions quite typically feel it is most unfair that they are, for instance, kept under continuous scrutiny by the police; they may actually set out to get revenge on those unfortunate enough to be cast in a persecutory role. Suicide can occur when either type of persecutory delusion is present. When the patient has delusions of deserved persecution, he may commit suicide because he feels punishment is merited and necessary; the paranoid schizophrenic patient who feels unjustly persecuted may also commit suicide, but for a different reason: he sees in death an escape from an unmerited torment (cf. Case 15).

Patients with *grandiose delusions* kill themselves occasionally because they are convinced their extraordinary powers enable them to achieve remarkable feats beyond the ability of ordinary people. A young man intoxicated with a street drug, convinced he could fly, might leap off a high building. Similar deaths occur in delirious states as well as in certain manic and schizophrenic conditions. Possibly such deaths should be classed as accidental, not suicidal, because to all appearances such patients do not intend to end their lives. They probably more closely resemble the rare deaths of somnambulistic falls and "accidents."

Hallucinations often accompany delusions in suicidal states, but they may occur independently. I cannot state that hallucinations have been statistically proven to increase the risk of suicide in psychotic depression, but clinical experience indicates that such is the case. Persecutory hallucinations are common in schizoaffective patients; when the patient is feeling no hope of getting better, they are an ominous prognostic sign. *Persecutory voices* make the lives of many patients almost intolerable as they shout insults, mockery, and obscenities hour after hour. *Tactile hallucinations* are less commonly found in schizophrenia, although some paranoid patients suffer from humiliating explorations of genitalia and anus by invisible persecutors. These are more often encountered in deliria and other organic psychoses. *Command hallucinations* comprise an important subtype of persecutory hallucinations; the voices do not stop with simple hostile outpourings, but actually order the patient to commit suicide, sometimes specifically insisting he must jump off a roof or shoot himself.

Case 24. "Jack R., a 24-year-old unmarried man, complained on admission that he continually heard the voice of God telling him to kill himself. He said he lacked the 'guts' to do so, but, beginning at age 16, he had made four suicidal gestures . . . following periods of paranoid delusions and hallucinations previously diagnosed as acute exacerbations of chronic paranoid schizophrenia. . . . Jack had worked only two weeks in his life . . . he was very restless, and he had a flat affect and a mask-like face. He felt hated by everyone. . . . [Medicines] were prescribed, and the patient became quiet and withdrawn almost immediately. After two days, he reported that he was 'living in torture' and that he wished to die. Little change was noted until the fourth day, when he awoke pleasant, cooperative, and sociable. Half an hour after taking his morning medications he was found hanged by a belt from the curtain rod in his bathroom shower." (Salama 1982)

Unfortunately many patients, fearing what the examiner will think or wishing to conceal their suicidal intentions, keep delusional or hallucinatory experiences a secret. That the patient has suffered from delusions or hallucinations is often learned only after the suicide has taken place, sometimes from a diary or from a suicide note (Case 13). Careful mental state examination will often give a clue that the patient may be subject to these dangerous phenomena when the examiner learns he is suffering from a *formal disorder of cognition*, or a *thought disorder*.

The examiner should look closely for any disorder in the connectedness or the rate of the patient's thought. *Looseness of associations*, one of the fundamental marks of schizophrenia, is difficult to define; it is characterized by conceptual disconnectedness and by the putting together of manifestly unrelated ideas. It is more than that—the patient seems vague; he illogically switches off onto seemingly unrelated side issues. Thought is directed by alliterations, analogies, symbolic meanings, clang associations, and condensations. Words are used concretely, quixotically. There is no discernable purpose in the flow of ideas. A *clang association* is based on similarity of sounds, without regard for differences of meaning. *Stereotypy* is the constant repetition of any action, including certain words or phrases. *Echolalia* is the pathological repetitive imitation of the speech of another. *Klebendenken* refers to adhesive, perseverative thinking in which certain ideas or phrases seem senselessly attached to each other. *Disorders of the rate of thinking* (different from disorders in the rate of speech) include uncontrollably racing thoughts, or sporadic, stop-and-go thinking. *Blocking* is an abrupt interruption of thinking in the middle of a train of ideas. If the patient is speaking he may halt in mid-sentence and sit mutely for a moment or for longer, unable to explain what has happened. He will not ordinarily inform the examiner that he is having this kind of trouble unless asked about it. *Concretization* is the opposite of abstraction: specific detail is overemphasized; words do not represent fully differentiated, integrated concepts, but remain embedded in perceptual experience, relating very much to immediate sensation. We commonly test patients for concrete thinking by asking them to interpret common proverbs. A concrete interpretation of the proverb "People who live in glass houses shouldn't throw stones," given by a schizophrenic patient, was "They might break the glass."

Cognitive disturbances are extremely important to detect and notice, not only because they alert us to the possibility of covert delusional and hallucinatory phenomena, but for two other reasons as well. Concrete thinking in particular, implying as it does a disturbance in the capacity for abstract thinking, is typical of many patients who are simply unable to think through the consequences of suicide. "Going to sleep forever," an everyday phrase denoting death, especially among children, will be understood by a concrete thinker to mean exactly that. For him, "gone to join his ancestors" is not a metaphorical expression; it is a literal description of what happens when one dies.

Abstraction difficulties cause suicide in many young patients who have set their hopes on careers of intellect and learning. With the appearance of schizophrenia in late adolescence and young adulthood, students who had previously performed superbly may find themselves inexplicably unable to learn. They complain they cannot concentrate. The real nature of the difficulty is easy to overlook. Sometimes the thought disorder that lies at the root of the problem is very subtle, manifesting itself in the course of an interview with no more than one or two odd (loose) associations. Concretization will not be detected unless actively looked for, and may not be detectable at all without formal psychological testing, unless the patient is in experienced hands. Wrong diagnosis is all too common in these cases.

Frequently mild depression is the first sign of dementia praecox (schizophrenia); the patient may feel nervous. But he is not suffering from ordinary student anxiety or the mild depression that so commonly follows moving away from home and matriculating in a strange university away from family and friends. He is faced with a major deterioration in cognitive functioning that will cost him the capacity to work intellectually. Reassurance, benzodiazepene compounds, and tricyclic antidepressants may be uselessly prescribed. Heroic efforts to study harder follow, but the student fails and fails again. He begins to think he is stupid or lazy and blames himself. Until the correct diagnosis is made (sometimes it is delayed until obvious psychotic symptoms appear) the patient will be alone with his illness. Recognition of the primary thought disorder at least opens the way to explanation, the prescription of more appropriate drugs, and psychotherapeutic efforts to help the patient bear what unfortunately often proves unbearable in the long run. Students for whom intellectual success is the principal sustaining resource, and who are suicide vulnerable, may end their lives tragically in these circumstances.

Case 25. Mr. D., a 25-year-old unmarried graduate student in philosophy, complained of difficulty studying. After a promising undergraduate performance, he had been accepted for the doctoral program at an important university across the country from his home. He was seen at the student health services and found to be anxious and tearful, but seemed otherwise intact. In spite of supportive interviews and the prescription of mild tranquilizers, his work deteriorated. He became deeply depressed and without warning attempted to hang himself. Fortunately and most improbably he was discovered by a roommate who arrived home unexpectedly and rescued him. Not until he was seen on a psychiatric inpatient unit by a senior consultant was it recognized that Mr. D. had a subtle but definite associative disorder, and that the attempt at suicide could be understood because this specific cognitive disturbance cost him the one thing he valued about himself—outstanding intellectual performance.

Another disorder of cognition that concerns us in assessing suicidal potential is *delirium*, "a syndrome of impairment of consciousness along with intrusive abnormalities derived from the fields of perception and affect." Consciousness is not merely quantiatively reduced in delirium, but is qualitatively changed. The patient is absorbed in his own inner world, struggling with illusions, hallucinations, and delusions, driven on by powerful affective changes derived therefrom. Conscious awareness of external events is disturbed, and psychomotor activity is usually increased in the form of restless and excited behavior. Its intensity fluctuates, and its content will manifest a fluid clinical picture (Lishman 1978).

Delirium occurs in a large variety of acute organic reactions; it frequently appears in elderly patients admitted to general hospitals for any number of illnesses. These facts are widely appreciated; that suicide occurs with increased frequency in delirious states is not. The delusions and hallucinations to which delirious patients are subject can be quite terrifying, driving some to jump out of hospital windows, but others to commit despairing suicides not unlike those found in depressive psychoses. Delirious patients whose verbalizations suggest despairing or frightening persecutory trends should be watched closely. Suicides of this sort sometimes take place in LSD intoxications (Keeler 1967).

In the course of collecting the patient's history and examining the mental state it will be possible to estimate to some degree whether the patient is able or willing to develop a reasonable rapport. If rapport can be established, the patient may be able to form a therapeutic alliance and revive his dimming hope that some improvement is possible. The patient who remains withdrawn, disinterested, guarded, and suspicious should arouse the greater concern. Indeed, it has been demonstrated that the patient who repudiates the hospital staff, remains aloof and critical of their efforts to help him while yet demanding relief and comfort is the more likely to commit suicide. Those others who are able to make relationships and to perceive the staff as persons of good will trying to help have a better outlook. The dependent-dissatisfied patient should worry us (Farberow 1970; Virkkunen 1976).

Having taken a history of the present crisis and systematically examined the patient's mental state, the clinician is in a position to specify what has failed in the patient's emotional world, how his sustaining resources have been compromised, what symptoms he has developed, and how these have further compromised his position. The examiner can integrate with this information what he has learned about the patient's immediate reaction to the situation; he can notice how depressed the patient has become, estimate whether or not he is preparing for suicidal action and with what degree of lethal intent. Furthermore, he will have an idea about the degree of hopelessness and the patient's capacity to make a relationship of trust. He will know whether certain disturbances of cognition are present that bode ill. He will also want to study how the patient has adapted to stress in the past. Past patterns of reaction are likely to repeat when past stresses reoccur. A grasp of the past history will refine and balance the preliminary formulation which has been made by integrating the information and observations already at hand.

Past History

We may look to the patient's previous psychiatric history to teach us whether he is a person critically reliant on external sustaining resources in order to maintain his equilibrium; when deprived of them, is he subject to primitive affect floods and ego regressions that put him in danger of suicide?

Begin by listing the times when the patient has felt most tried throughout his life. Learn what you can about what provoked each occasion of stress, what the patient did to help himself, to whom he turned for help, whether he required

professional attention, and whether hospital admission was necessary. You can then systematically review each period of crisis
to formulate a judgment about the patient's reliance on external
sustaining resources.

Most suicide crisis situations are triggered by losses. What
has thrown the patient out of balance in each past situation?
On what sort of person, activity, or personal attribute has he
characteristically relied in order to maintain self-respect and
inner comfort? Some strength is implied when the patient has
demonstrated the ability to make a variety of different kinds
of emotional investment to buttress himself. The man who rests
secure in the love of his wife and his friends, derives appropriate
satisfaction from interesting work, and takes pride in his skill
at racquet sports is obviously better protected from crisis than
another who claims only one of these.

How has the patient reacted to each past crisis? As we have
noticed previously, individuals dealt the same cruel blow may
respond very differently, according to the endowment each
brings to the situation. Suppose a patient has responded to a
critical bereavement with sadness, a temporary loss of interest
in others and in work, and weeping, but not with excessive
self blame—he has grieved. Another with a past bereavement
may have shown all the same marks of grief, but additionally,
he may have blamed himself, withdrawn, lost weight, felt agitated, and wished he were dead. This patient responded with
a clinical depression. Offered psychiatric treatment, he accepted
it gratefully, formed a good therapeutic alliance, and recovered.
A third added to the features of clinical depression experiences
of depersonalization, active suicidal daydreaming, and morbid
self-contempt; he was unable to remain by himself for more
than a few minutes because of eerie feelings of aloneness. In
addition, he experienced fits of uncontrollable rage after drinking
in which he smashed furniture. Offered a psychiatric interview,
he rejected it, remarking that it wouldn't do any good anyway,

he was hopeless. Such a history implies there has been a past suicidal crisis.

Previous psychiatric diagnoses are of obvious importance; statistical studies have shown that patients bearing certain diagnoses are at graver risk than others. A good grasp of the statistical background is indispensable; it will not show whether a given patient is dangerously suicidal or not, but it will inform clinical judgment as one weighs the importance and availability of sustaining resources for each case that comes for evaluation.

Every study shows that a very high proportion of successful suicides takes place among patients with diagnoses, past or present, of major affective disorders. Out of every hundred successful suicides, between a third and two-thirds will have borne diagnoses in this class (Robins 1981; Barraclough 1974; Dorpat 1960). Furthermore, about 15 percent of patients who have suffered serious depressive illnesses die by suicide (Miles 1977; Winokur 1975). Deluded depressed patients are five times more likely to commit suicide than depressed patients without delusions (Roose 1983).

Chronic alcoholics are at high risk also; about a fourth of completed suicides fall into this class. Robins (1981) noticed that suicide in alcoholics was especially likely to be triggered by the loss of an important relationship. Suicide usually occurs late in the alcoholic career and is associated with factors otherwise identified with high risk, such as increasing age, physical illness, and previous attempts. About 10 percent of opiate addicts will die by suicide.

Schizophrenics comprise between 2 and 11 percent of the successful suicides. More than half the suicides in inpatient settings, however, are schizophrenic (Niskanen 1974). When schizophrenic illness is complicated with depressive features, the risk of suicide is comparable to that in patients with major affective disorders (Schuttler 1976). Patients who have been ill for some time and who have had a relapse or two are at particular risk. 80 percent of schizophrenic suicides are men, and these patients differ from those with affective disorders in that they do not wait until middle or late life to do it—the mean age at suicide was about twenty-six in one series (Roy 1982). Schizophrenic patients who kill themselves typically have high personal standards for performance, the achievement of which has been rendered impossible by the illness. Feeling inadequate in relation to their goals and fearing further disintegration, they are increasingly likely to despair of the future as psychotic episodes recur (Drake 1984).

About 5 percent of patients with a sociopathic diagnosis die by suicide (perhaps there are 2000 such deaths in the United States annually, many of which must occur in jails). Most jail suicides occur in young men of whom many have made previous attempts. Hanging is the usual method.

Has the patient made previous suicide attempts? If so, under what circumstances, and with what degree of ambivalence about living or dying? The answers to these questions are critically important aspects of the previous psychiatric history. Try to assess the gravity of each past attempt according to the scheme given at the beginning of this chapter.

Our understanding of the relationship between past attempted suicide and future committed suicide remains rather unsatisfactory, but some generalizations are possible. To begin with, we know that between 10 and 20 percent of previous attempters go on to kill themselves; three-quarters of the successful suicides will have made at least two previous attempts before going on to complete the act (Ettlinger 1964). Multiple attempts bode a future suicidal death. A number of factors have been identified in those who have made a previous attempt that are associated with probable future suicide (Dorpat 1967):

older age	men more than women
gravity of previous	multiple attempts
attempt	not married
living alone	poor physical health
psychosis	lethal method used before
left a suicide note	infrequent use of health
unemployed or retired	agencies
from a broken home	

An examination of this list suggests circumstances without sustaining resources. Old age, living alone, and being unmarried all imply the loss or lack of supportive others. Unemployment and retirement make it unlikely that sustaining work is available. Poor physical health and the infrequent use of health agencies bespeak not only illness, but hopelessness about getting better. Other items suggest that the patients at hazard are in their characters disposed to despair—serious and multiple previous attempts with lethal methods imply a readiness to surrender; psychosis implies loss of reality testing and vulnerability to primitive fantasies about death.

Patients with histories of grave previous attempts who plainly meant to end their lives will commonly have suffered at that time from depression, despair, and social isolation. These closely resemble those who succeed in suicide. When such a person appears for the evaluation of a fresh suicidal crisis, great care must be exercised (Dorpat 1963; Lester 1979).

Family History

The patient's *family history* needs to be examined from a developmental perspective, but statistical studies can alert us to specific family phenomena that are associated with increased suicide risk. Have other members of the family committed suicide or attempted it? Was the family broken by divorce or death? Was there child abuse? These findings in a patient's past can dispose him to suicide.

In collecting the family history, recall that in recent years the suicide rate has been rising in young black urban males, and that American Indians and Eskimos commit suicide more frequently than the general population. It seems probable that poverty and its consequences, coupled with frequent family disruption, lie behind these statistics.

A family history of suicide significantly increases the risk for an attempt at suicide in patients across a wide diagnostic spectrum (Roy 1983). There is some suggestion a genetic factor may be at work here; twin studies have shown that in nine cases where both twins committed suicide, each set of twins was identical (Tsuang 1977; Rainer 1985). Environmental influences must be taken into account as well, because the association between attempted suicide and parental death in childhood and adolescence is an established one. Parental loss in childhood sensitizes some patients so that in adulthood later losses become intolerably painful and may precipitate suicide attempts (Birtchnell 1970; Lester 1976). A significant number of children who behave suicidally has lost a parent before the age of twelve.

If the loss of family members is commonplace in suicide attempters, it is particularly frequent in the sickest cases. In a series of fifty severely suicidal patients, 95 percent had experienced the death or loss of parents, siblings, and/or mates; in three-quarters of the cases, the losses had taken place before the end of adolescence. A fourth of the patients had a family history of suicide (Moss 1956).

When a parent dies of suicide significant developmental problems are imposed on a child, and depressive and suicidal psychopathology may result. Parental suicide during latency is a particularly serious matter for those children who have not satisfactorily resolved the earlier developmental issues of separation-individuation. Ego and superego development may be deformed. When the surviving parent's mourning or depression interferes with open discussion in the family about death, as is commonly the case, the trauma is heightened. Parental suicide can stimulate suicidal fantasy and impulses if the child identifies with the dead parent (Pfeffer 1981, 1981a). Suicide is sometimes an effort to complete identification with a dead person (Hendrick 1940); in others, it is an attempt to rejoin someone (typically a sustaining resource) beyond the grave. Zilboorg was convinced that the death of a close relative during the Oedipal period or during its adolescent revival gives rise to "identification with death" if the person who dies is hated and his death is wished for. He took this to be a strong predisposing factor to later suicide; he commented that a number of patients attempt or commit suicide exactly on the anniversary of the death of a person who died when the patient was in the Oedipal or adolescent years.

Case 26. "A girl in Boston committed suicide by jumping from a window. She was 21. The story of the relatives was the usual one, as follows: 'Who would have thought of it? She appeared perfectly normal, she was very cheerful, went out with a friend shopping and bought herself a new dress. One would never have suspected it. . . .'

If you review a great many suicidal cases you will find that for 24 to 48 hours before they commit the act there is a tendency on the part of these individuals . . . to dress up, to put on their best clothes, to look wonderfully well—and they are very friendly. . . . I will mention that no suicide among primitive races is every [sic] committed in any other than a ceremonial way. Before the act is committed the suicidal boy or girl or the woman or man goes into his tent and puts on ceremonial clothes, occasionally he climbs a tree and makes a speech, and then goes to his death. This girl in Boston bought herself a new dress, and she appeared cheerful. There is a tinge of the ceremonial. If it is true that there is a tinge of the ceremonial in it, then this death must be related to the death of a close relative, because the ceremony of joining in death and jumping on the funeral pyre is well known.

A friend of mine wrote me from Boston about this case. He told me the story and asked, 'What ceremony is this?' I asked him to give me the history of the girl, and gradually in about 2 weeks the following was uncovered: The girl's mother died 7 years previously, when the girl was 14. The girl started menstruating at the age of 14, a very short time before her mother died. Toward this information my colleague was very friendly but very scientific. He said that my theory of dates was very interesting but that this girl did not die on the same date that her mother died. He said, 'If only this had happened, your theory would have been corroborated.' So we went back 7 years and calculated the day of the week when this girl's mother died. We found it was Friday, and, what is more, it was Good Friday. The days of the month did not coincide, but the days of the week did. . . . On Thursday she bought herself a dress, and the next day she jumped out of a window, 7 years to the day after her mother's death." (Zilboorg 1975)

(Zilboorg offered no comment on the symbolism implied by a Good Friday suicide, but the implication is obvious. Christ shared the last supper with his apostles on Maundy Thursday, died on Good Friday, and rose again on Easter. It is likely that the "girl from Boston" imagined she would rise again like Christ to rejoin her mother on Easter in the life of the world to come.)

This Good Friday suicide reminds us that identification with a dead parent is a strong force in the direction of suicide. Nikolai Gogol (1809–1852), the Russian writer, was one of five children who survived in a family into which twelve were born. His father died during Nikolai's adolescence after a long illness. Gogol starved himself to death at the age of forty-three, remarking that his father had died at the same age, and of the "same disease" (Kanzer 1953; Pollock 1970). Sylvia Plath, the contemporary poet who committed suicide in 1963 at the age of thirty, lost her father shortly after her eighth birthday. Her poetry, distinctly sadomasochistic in tone, is scattered with allusions to her father and his entomological work (bees). In one of the poems, "Daddy," written after her almost fatal attempt in 1953, she says,

> I was ten [sic] when they buried you.
> At twenty I tried to die
> And get back, back, back to you.
> I thought even the bones would do.
>   (Plath 1961)

Developmental History

Orphaned children are likely to develop depressive illnesses when they grow to adulthood, and to have suicidal difficulties as well. Other childhood suffering can increase the likelihood of adult suicide. Goldney (1981) showed that young women who attempt suicide are more likely than a set of controls to report a childhood broken home, frequent parental quarreling, frequent conflict with the parents, and dislike of the parents. Furthermore, it is well established that children who have been abused physically or sexually are likely to become self-mutilators later in life—behavior of this sort seems to be a learned pattern originating in early traumatic experiences with hostile parents (Green 1978). Self-mutilative patients frequently attempt suicide, of course; their hostile, disturbed behavior and sadomasochistic preoccupations undoubtedly relate to psychological and physical abuse in childhood (Carroll 1980; Roy 1978; Green 1978). These findings, well documented in the literature, invite attention to the patient's developmental history. Experiences of the sort just reviewed do not foster development of the healthy mental structures necessary for anxiety mastery and self-esteem regulation. Inasmuch as suicidal patients have great difficulty with separation-individuation, self-respect, anxiety mastery, the regulation of aggression, and reality testing, pay special attention to the first six years of life. Ego and superego development on which these functions depend occurs during that time—in the pre-Oedipal and Oedipal eras. In later years look for symptoms that suggest these emotionally vital functions have not developed adequately. The breaking up of a home or the loss of a parent because of divorce or illness, but especially suicide, is important at any point, but particularly in the first six years and later in adolescence, when Oedipal struggles revive.

If a child is to master separation anxiety, learn to tolerate solitude with reasonable comfort, and develop some resilience in maintaining self-regard, he needs empathic, consistent love and care from his mother in the first three years (or from the person who substitutes for her). Thus it is important to find out what sort of mothering experiences the patient had early in life. Of course, early developmental history is difficult to collect, but persistence and inquiries addressed to older siblings or senior relatives can sometimes elicit valuable information.

Was the mother available, loving and consistent? Was she interested in feeding, cleaning, clothing, and soothing her child? The development of a well integrated sense of self probably depends on the organizing experience of having a competent mother attend to the various parts of her baby's body according to its needs from moment to moment. Children whose mothers naturally and easily keep them comfortable, fed, and clean grow up wanting to keep themselves in the same condition—without such mothering they may prove indifferent to their physical welfare and even have difficulty feeling at home in their own skins.

What about the mother's attitudes toward the child's emotional needs? Did she show that these had any importance to her? If not, the child will not only have remained chronically emotionally distressed, but probably will have failed to develop any confidence that he can do anything to comfort or soothe himself. Patients who have not been loved, comforted, and looked after as small children may grow up with the capacity to love, comfort, and care for others, but they will have enormous difficulty in doing these things for themselves. They will need others to do for them what their mothers did not if they are to carry on (exterior sustaining resources).

Watch for mother-child interactions that were predominantly sadomasochistic in tone, in which the child submitted to the mother's controlling, invasive attitude. Such experiences often give rise to confusion over body ownership. The mother will be idealized but unconsciously hated in later life (conscious aggressive impulses will not be allowed by the mother-like superego), and the patient will be submissive and low in self-esteem. See what memories the patient has about the toilet and bathroom. Was mother so determined on regular defecation that she dosed with laxatives and forced enemas?

Early kitchen memories of patients are often instructive. A woman with a history of multiple suicide attempts told me that her mother was extremely solicitous about her meals; when her mother was afraid she was not eating properly, she would fretfully and naggingly try to force her little girl to swallow. Battles followed in which both the patient and her mother would panic, and food would be thrown about the room. The mother wanted to feed her because she was afraid that if the patient did not eat, she would fall ill and die. The giving and taking of food was not a loving experience. This patient had no memory of ever being offered an ice cream cone, a cookie, or anything nice to eat as an expression of motherly love.

Case 27. Mary, an 18-year-old girl, drove her car down a steep embankment, suffered severe injuries, and nearly died in a lethally-intended suicide attempt. She was dependent on and completely cowed by a dominating, cold mother about whom she was totally unable to entertain the slightest negative thought. There was a sadomasochistic battle between the two over who owned Mary's body. Mary commented on her mother's rough, "no nonsense" handling of her niece, remarking that the mother would have been a good animal trainer, but a bad child raiser. She told her psychoanalyst, "I always thought feelings should be neat and tidy"; before treatment she had been unable to tolerate ambivalent feelings, and her severe constriction of affect and activity were linked to fears of losing bladder and bowel control. Extreme dependency and submission defended against fury at the mother; "If I'm angry at someone else I still have mother, but if I'm angry at mother then I'm all alone." Later in the treatment it emerged that the wrecked car had been the mother's favorite possession [except possibly Mary]. (Novick 1984)

Liking one's own body is an important barrier to self-injury. Usually by the middle of the first year babies have experienced enough pleasurable well-being to evolve some sense of a primitive, discrete body-self whose comfort they want to preserve. They do not bite or bang themselves, they protest when hurt, they seek and accept comfort and welcome feeling good again. The gradual accretion of memories coupling pleasant body experiences with the mother's loving ministrations, protection, and soothing builds up a bodily self-liking that creates a lasting barrier to self-injury.

Not all children complete these important developmental steps. Illness or physical distress the mother cannot alleviate or unfortunate handling can get in the way. Furman (1984) remarked,

When the parent actually inflicts hurt on children's bodies through rough care, in anger, excitement, or by way of punishment, such children cannot develop a proper liking for their bodies. They identify with the parental mistreatment of their bodies and may even come to enjoy and seek pain and discomfort in pathological gratification instead of avoiding and protesting such experiences. Early signs of such a development can be seen in not complaining when hurt, not seeking help and comfort, delay in learning to avoid common dangers, repeated injuries, accident proneness, self-hurting "comfort" habits, such as headbanging, violent scratching, hair pulling, injurious masturbatory activities, and in provocations to physical attack and punishment.

Children's failure to develop their protective bodily self-love is paralleled by a failure in the concomitant step of differentiation between self and object. When their raw and/or sexualized aggression is directed against themselves, it may therefore also represent aggression to the parental figures, vengeance upon them, or excited violent interaction with them. The more shaky and inadequate the earliest loving bodily investment, the more prone are patients to self-damaging and suicidal actions. . . . This includes not only active self-hurting but passive inability to care for themselves, which can be just as life threatening.

Excessive early sadomasochistic excitement can lead to primitive fixations to which vulnerable patients may regress under stress. Identification of experiences favoring this kind of fixation is an important part of surveying the past history.

Were there intermittent separations? Sometimes a child may be farmed out to other relatives and may feel repudiated by his parents. Sometimes one discovers that the mother has been hostile and rejecting in fact, abusing the child with verbal devaluation, sarcasm, and attacks on the first sprouts of sexual self-esteem (some mothers deride their sons for being "sissified"). Was she prone to rages and tirades, slapping, or beating? Other mothers will withdraw into haughty silences that last for days. Maternal depression or psychosis can emotionally isolate a young child and leave him feeling utterly alone. Did the mother make suicide threats or attempts? Was there a divorce, a separation because of a long illness or other cause? Did the mother die?

Similar information is gathered about the father. Was he supportive, kind, interested in his child, consistent with discipline, or indifferent and rejecting? Perhaps he was usually absent, or if at home, aloof or frightening. Did he approve of the patient as a child, acknowledging achievements and giving appropriate praise, or was he never satisfied? Was he abusive to his wife or children, did he drink excessively? Was he ill, depressed, psychotic? Did he abandon the family?

Were there early surgical and medical illnesses that put the patient into the hospital away from his mother? Small children often experience hospitalization, with its attendant immobilization and instrumentation, as parental abandonment followed by attack from strangers; separation mastery becomes more difficult after such experiences. Were there psychosomatic illnesses such as asthma, an eating disorder, unexplained recurrent vomiting, undocumented "allergy"? Such ailments are sometimes expressions of separation anxiety. Asthma in particular and respiratory problems in general, to the extent they give rise to sensations of choking to death, may be accompanied by anxiety of desperate, traumatic proportions. Asthma attacks sometimes arise in children who fear being left alone, so that asthma both expresses and aggravates separation anxiety. The over-anxious mother excessively fretful about her child's health sometimes makes it impossible for normal separation to take place; adults who as children have been fussed over in this way tend to view the world as dangerous and themselves as fragile; they need the intervention of others (external sustaining resources) to maintain some degree of inner peace.

In the years before school were there signs of emotional unrest? Was the patient a headbanger, accident prone, apt to run into the street or otherwise get into dangerous situations? When a separation impended did he fly into rages and have tantrums or attacks of panic and weeping?

Pay particular attention to separations, deaths, and other losses. Try to learn how the patient reacted to these. If the parents were unable to meet his emotional needs, were other adults available to lend support, soothing, and validation? Other relatives, especially grandparents, are often important substitute or auxiliary parents. From the child's viewpoint sometimes someone other than the biological, "official" mother is the emotional mother in fact. When the de facto mother dies the effect can be devastating, but the full import of such a loss cannot be appreciated unless the examiner has established the identity of the de facto, emotional mother. When grandparents or other relatives have been frequently in the home, try to ascertain what their emotional importance to the patient was as a child, when they died, and how he responded.

If the patient was adopted, when and under what circumstances was he parted from his mother? Was there a foster home placement, or many such? Rapid adoption in early infancy is less likely to be developmentally injurious than disruptions of the mothering experience later on. It is not unusual to hear of shifting about from one foster home to another in the childhood of a suicidal patient.

When there are siblings, sort them out chronologically; try to see at what point in the patient's development the younger ones arrived in the family and how the patient reacted. The appearance of a new infant may be experienced, especially by children who are not substantially through the separation-individuation phase, as a rejection. Were foster children or perhaps cousins brought into the family? The bringing in and the sending away of foster children heightens separation anxiety and can reinforce abandonment fears.

The development of phobias and fresh intolerance for being left alone after the arrival of a new baby suggests anxiety of this sort. Miscarriages and sibling deaths should be noted carefully. It is not uncommon for a child to feel deeply guilty should a hated sibling die. Many suicidal patients believe they should have died instead of a sibling, and, rightly or wrongly, are convinced that the mother or father would have preferred that the patient die instead of the more beloved brother or sister.

Nursery school and kindergarten are the usual first separations from home a child experiences. How did the patient respond?

Was he able to integrate himself with other children with reasonable confidence, or were there panics, tantrums, and resistance? So-called "school phobia" is really not a phobia at all, though children who suffer from it are certainly afraid. What they fear is not so much the school; it is being separated from home and abandoned at school that terrifies them. A number of children are so distressed at the prospect of leaving home that they vomit every morning when the hour for setting out arrives.

How was the transition to elementary school negotiated? How did the patient take to his teachers and they to him? Did he progress normally? What were his academic strengths and weaknesses? Was he nervous? A child with separation anxiety may contrive an unusual number of small sicknesses by means of which he remains at home to watch his mother to be sure she does not vanish from his life.

Another childhood indication of poor separation mastery is intolerance for going away to summer camp. A child of nine or ten should be able to go to camp without suffering excessive "homesickness." When a twelve or fifteen year old cannot stay in camp because of separation distress, future trouble may be in store.

How did the patient relate to the other children and to his teachers? Signs of sadomasochistic fixations may arise in the elementary school years. Latency-age boys tend to be somewhat sadistic in the course of normal development, but they should not stand out as excessively so. Masochistic behavior in school is worth attention. Did the patient provoke attacks, insults, rejections, humiliations? Did he provoke his teachers and then complain that they disliked him? Some children are prone to brood about dying, and occasionally they threaten suicide. Rarely, they attempt it. Childhood suicide rumination, threatening, and behavior should be enquired after.

In adolescence (and before) look for the development of unrealistic and perfectionistic self-ideals. Some youngsters can become profoundly self-critical if they earn anything less than "straight As" on every report card. I recall one wretched fourth grader who was so upset each time he made a mistake in his arithmetic that he burst into tears and had to leave the schoolroom; in adulthood there were depressive difficulties at the core of which lay a demanding superego. A young athlete who drives himself to foolish extremes and is implacably self-contemptuous when his performance does not come up to champion-like expectations has similar difficulty. Such attitudes to school work and athletic performances are likely to be carried forward into the work life of the patient as maturation proceeds.

With the arrival of adolescence, suicide attempts become much more frequent, as does suicidal daydreaming. These details are obviously important when discovered in the patient's past history. Was there disruptive school behavior, delinquency, truancy, or dropping out of school?

In contrast to normal experimentation, was there a pattern of drug or alcohol abuse? Did the patient show signs of impulsivity? Was there a history of self-destructive sexual behavior? Pronounced mood swings often appear in adolescence, sometimes sufficient in intensity to satisfy the criteria for a major depression or hypomanic attack.

How did the patient respond to leaving home for college? Was the patient unable to leave? When an adolescent has not sufficiently separated from the parents, personal, family, and social expectations that he will move to a distant university and take up studies as an autonomous adult can sometimes trigger a first suicide attempt or a psychosis; remaining at home can represent an effort, often not successful, to avert psychiatric catastrophe.

Bear in mind that youngsters continue to develop through adolescence and that many who have shown signs of separation intolerance, masochistic trends, and excessive dependency will master their problems sufficiently to escape full suicide vulnerability in adult life. When such problems are pronounced in adolescence, however, especially when there are frank suicidal trends, they will usually continue to find expression later. It is the adult and later adolescent history that will show to what degree the patient is reliant on external sustaining resources and vulnerable to suicidal ego regression when deprived of them.

Occupational History

Examination of the patient's occupational history will tell when the patient began to work and how he felt about his work; it will disclose changes in occupation and the reasons for changing. Relationships with work associates and superiors also need investigation. This part of the past history will show how valuable the patient's work has been as a source of self-respect; from it one can learn how the patient has responded in the past when work has not gone well. A precocious overinvestment in after school jobs may be a healthy sign in some boys and girls, but it may also represent a grim self-attitude with an early need to achieve a sustaining external resource in the form of a job. The patient, feeling worthless himself, renders himself more self-acceptable (superego acceptable) by identifying himself with first-class work performance. A tendency to worry excessively about one's work, to react in an anxious way when it does not progress smoothly, and to be unrealistically preoccupied with being fired or dismissed is suggestive of primitive pathology. It is important to notice how the patient has responded in the past when laid off, promoted, or dismissed (for whatever cause).

Patients who repeatedly fail at work may, of course, do so for a variety of reasons. With regard to suicide vulnerability, one should look for two phenomena in particular. The first is masochistic character pathology in which the patient, consciously or unconsciously, repeatedly causes himself to fail, provoking employers to the point of dismissal. Some patients feel so unworthy that they will not allow themselves work commensurate with talent, ability, or training. Convinced they merit no other, they compulsively choose uninteresting or menial work. Often they are afraid to try truly worthwhile work because they are convinced that failing at it would be inevitable.

A second reason for repeated work failure is paranoid pathology, often fairly subtle, that makes collaboration with others too frightening to tolerate. Some patients are convinced that co-workers hate them, and conspire to do them some disservice or to get them fired. They may be convinced that they are the subject of constant malicious gossip. Such an attitude often invites the very behavior from others that the patient fears, so that no workplace is tolerable. One may suspect in such patients that a disposition toward profound self-contempt is being managed by projection, the paranoid attitude serving to ward off substantial depression.

Social History

The patient's adult social history will include investigation of friendships, sexual history, marital history, religious practices, and personal habits.

The patient who has few or no friends, or who has a history of making intense attachments to others and then breaking them off in bitterness and disillusionment, will more likely prove vulnerable to suicidal crises than another who has a life-long pattern of stable, deep, and loving attachments to a number of other people who return his affection and respect. A pattern of a long and deep attachment to only one other person should alert one to the possibility that the relationship in question may be a vital sustaining resource that is keeping the patient out of trouble. What reaction has the patient shown in the past when such a relationship was troubled? To react with depression when a valued friend moves across the country is one thing; to brood about death or daydream about hanging oneself is another.

Patients with borderline personality disorders (many of whom simultaneously satisfy the diagnostic criteria for major affective illnesses) typically seek out a series of special friendships from which they hope to derive the comforting and soothing they cannot provide themselves. These attachments usually begin with great hope and idealization and end suddenly when the new friend fails to meet the unrealistic hopes with which the patient invested him. The breaking up of these relationships is often accompanied by an upsurge of very painful affect, depersonalization, and self-hate, which can culminate in self-mutilation or a suicide attempt.

Remember that some people prefer animals over human friends. Is there a life pattern of unusual devotion to pets with signs of serious trouble when they die?

Has the patient relied on sexual contact for reassurance he is adequate and worthwhile? Some women become promiscuous in adolescence because sexual contact brings admiring attention and appreciation from men that was never available at home in a dependable way. Both sexes can rely on sexual contact (homosexual or heterosexual) to relieve feelings of aloneness or to ward off psychosis. Phenomena of this sort are important to seek out in taking the sexual history. Some patients who experience difficulty in maintaining self-object differentiation may not be able to tolerate sexual intimacy with others because intercourse and orgasm threaten disintegration and fusion with the partner. Intolerance of reasonable sexual frustration, deep fears of sexual intercourse, promiscuous behavior, and sadomasochistic perversions should alert one to the possibility that the patient may be vulnerable to a suicidal crisis.

The marital history will show to what extent the patient is dependent on the love and approval of the mate to maintain self-regard and inner peace. An excessively submissive, clinging attitude alternating with rages and withdrawal suggests that the patient is trying to keep his balance by using husband or wife as a sustaining resource. Further evidence that the marital partner serves this function will be provided when pathological jealousy, intolerance for brief separations, a constant need for reassurance, and panicky responses to the partner's minor illnesses are discovered. If there has been a divorce or death of the spouse and the patient, in the absence of another exterior sustaining resource, has weathered the bereavement without evidence of serious crisis, reasonably good self-sustaining mental structures are implied.

Patients should be asked about religious faith and practice, the examiner remaining alert for evidence of idiosyncrasies of belief and religious experience. Suicide vulnerable individuals are likely to have profound sadomasochistic dispositions, a trait that will color this area as well as others. God the Father, Christ, the Holy Ghost, the Blessed Virgin, the Angels and the Saints will often be so transformed in the minds of these patients as to startle the examiner. Far from being loving and kind, they emerge as diabolical in their capriciousness, perfectionism, vengefulness, and austerity. The child's primitive perceptions of his parents will have been applied to divine figures, and as the child once trembled before them, the worshipping adult may now cringe before Heaven in fearful, placatory prayer. St. Augustine, after all, declared that Hell was the experience of being sent away forever from the presence of God. In peaceful times, however, the patient may feel that he is in divine favor and that God or one of his Heavenly messengers is close and protecting. When the patient feels abandoned or when, despairing of ever pleasing God, he turns away from the Church, a suicidal crisis may develop. It is well to go into some detail with deeply religious patients about what they have experienced in crises of belief.

What are the patient's favorite recreations and pastimes? Remember that some adults live only to exercise or for some prized activity, perhaps mountain climbing or chess playing. If the patient seems devoted to some special cause or endeavor, try to find out how he has responded in the past if his pursuit has been interrupted for some reason.

Medical History

Finally, the patient's *medical history* should be investigated. This will disclose any past tendency to turn against his body as an enemy when it no longer performs as he wishes (the aging professor in Case 21 viewed his body as a potential prison with the approach of illness and old age, as did Seneca); examination of the social and work consequences of illness can show us how the patient responds to disruptions in his relationships to important sustaining resources. We may also learn to what extent the patient will use ill health to claim special attention and care from others whom he feels might otherwise remain indifferent to him.

Summary

From the past history the examiner will be able to form a good estimate of his patient's past reliance for emotional balance on sustaining resources outside the structure of his own ego-superego. The past history will show not only the degree of such reliance, but the characteristic difficulty into which the patient falls when deprived of a necessary sustaining resource. Furthermore, it will disclose what kind of sustaining resource the patient must have in order to keep in balance. Some have a special predeliction for work in this respect; others require pets, others yet, athletic activities. The past history will indicate whether the patient is sustaining resource reliant, what class of sustaining resource he must have in order to keep in equilibrium, and how he has responded in the past when deprived of the necessary support—that is, whether he is suicide vulnerable. The history of the present illness will have helped identify what sustaining resources in the present have failed and what symptoms the patient is developing at the moment in response to their loss. The mental state examination allows some measure of the current subjective distress, and coupled with the history of the present illness, can teach to what degree the patient is slipping into an ego-regression that will lead to suicide. The integration of this information comprises the psychodynamic formulation of suicide risk. A case example illustrating the use of psychodynamic formulation appears at the end of the next chapter.

Psychodynamic formulation not only provides a rational basis for estimating the degree of hazard when a patient who may be suicidal comes for clinical evaluation. It is also the foundation on which treatment planning should be built, including decisions for admission and discharge from psychiatric inpatient facilities. Formulation is the basis as well of intelligent psychoanalytic psychotherapy of suicidal patients, but these matters are outside the scope of this book.

5.

Pitfalls in Estimating Suicide Danger

Even in highly reputable psychiatric departments the necessity for formulation is often overlooked, and as a consequence, preventable suicides occasionally occur. In such cases, the history and mental status are put away in a file drawer without careful analysis or any attempt at formulation. Treatment proceeds, often guided by superficial shifts in the patient's mental state. Critically significant matters that a formulation would place in the center of the clinical stage receive casual or no attention. Shifts in family attitudes, the impact of a change at work, the arrival of an important anniversary, the departure of a ward attendant to whom the patient had formed an attachment— these and scores of other little but possibly vital details are overshadowed in the rush and bustle of hospital life. Staff meetings, pharmacology discussions, and other important activities make it difficult to think each case through carefully.

Misuse of the Mental State Examination

As a result, false assumptions are often made. The significance of mild yet critical shifts in the mental state is overlooked. At a major psychiatric center connected to a prestigious medical school, the following suicide took place some years ago:

Case 28. Dianne B., a depressed young inpatient with a history of an episodic schizophrenic illness, exhibited anew some loosened associations. This the staff noted, but nobody took the time systematically to fully reinvestigate her mental state. They overlooked the implication that delusions or hallucinations might accompany this fresh cognitive difficulty. A few hours later Miss B. slipped away and jumped from the hospital roof. She was carried into the emergency room downstairs. Dying, she described a chorus of commanding hallucinatory voices— "Jump!, jump off the roof!" they had cried. Formulation had been ignored and the presence of hallucinogenic hostile introjects had not previously been suspected.

This tragedy illustrates the first common mistake in assessing the present danger of a suicide that arises from the misuse of the mental status examination: it is not carried out systematically and completely and is not repeated from time to time when shifts in the patient's clinical or personal situation take place (especially shifts in the availability of important other people). The mental state examination can be quite useful in detecting early ego regression, particularly when it is used in connection with the case formulation. Formulation may suggest that regression is likely (perhaps the patient has sustained a new loss). The mental state examination and special attention to evidence of lost reality testing, cognitive disturbances, and decay of self-object differentiation can alert the examiner to trouble when it first begins to emerge.

Perhaps the most common error in assessing, managing and treating suicidal patients is an over reliance on what is suggested by the manifest mood. It is easy to trust the most obvious; mood completely determines many decisions. The history and its integration with the rest of the mental state are simply set aside. For example, some patients are seriously suicidal without appearing depressed, and some depressed patients with suicidal ideation may not be in dangerous condition.

The clinical adage that the depressed patient who is getting better may be especially likely to commit suicide is hoary with age, but it is not helpful. Obviously, most people who have been depressed and are getting better are not actively suicidal. Yet depression sometimes lifts when a patient decides to do away with himself. Despair does not, and despair is a state of mind not coexistent or congruent with depressed affect in all respects.

Many people commit suicide who are not clinically depressed. It has been known for years that schizophrenic individuals are suicide vulnerable, and so are many others who show few if any of the classic marks of depression such as weight loss, retardation of motor activity and speech, sleeplessness, or other vegetative signs.

In some hospitals the decision to admit or to discharge from the psychiatric department is likely to be based almost entirely on the mental state examination. When this is the practice, it is inevitable that a certain number of otherwise preventable suicides will take place. It is simply not true that the patient who looks better and talks better is necessarily safe from suicide.

Zilboorg (1936) observed years ago that many individuals who commit suicide are spiteful and angry in emotional attitude (see Cases 2 and 11), not depressed. Other suicides take place when the patient is under the sway of a terrifying delusional system so that the predominating affect in the mental state examination is terror (Cases 15, 24). Others yet may kill themselves in turmoil at the onset of psychosis or delirium because death seems preferable to the agony that accompanies self-disintegration. The mental state examination of such patients will reveal acute and gross disorganization of thought and marked affective lability.

The patient with a "smiling depression" may also be in grave suicidal danger. Under a superficially bright mood may lie despair, concealed from view because the patient, fiercely independent, is determined never to acknowledge the need for support from anyone. Only by weighing the mental state examination against a careful formulation of character organization and an assessment of who is available as an external sustaining resource can one form a realistic judgment of the hazard of suicide.

As another example of the suicidal case whose mental state examination does not necessarily suggest danger, recall those patients who are emerging from paranoid psychosis (Case 14). It is clinically possible for such persons to move into severely suicidal states as paranoid, blaming attitudes give way to guilt and self-contempt.

Disorders of the mental state can not only be indicators of suicide potential (though poor predictors) but can provoke suicide as well. Some patients may be difficult to understand psychodynamically until a meticulous and systematic mental state examination is carried out. Just as errors can arise from ignoring certain aspects of the mental state and from emphasizing manifest mood to the exclusion of other data, suicide can take place when implications of the mental state examination are not appreciated in the light of the psychodynamic formulation.

There are, for instance, tragic people who recognize that they are psychotic and who become suicidally depressed in reaction to the discovery. These may attempt to conceal secret hallucinations or delusions from clinicians. This they may succeed in doing, but cognitive disturbances can often be detected if the patient is painstakingly and expertly examined.

Others cannot endure the pain of acknowledging a thought disorder or some other defect of mind such as a mild dementia. Suicides can take place in those who prize highly and lose an intact and effective capacity for clear thought, just as other individuals (certain athletes, for example) may become suicidal because they lose some highly prized bodily function. It is obvious in such cases that we cannot assess the degree of

suicidal danger without taking into account the subjective meaning to the patient of what has been lost (see Case 25).

Whenever one is examining a patient to assess suicide risk
it is essential to survey the mental content carefully for illusions
or secret delusions that may lead the patient into lethal behavior
in the false belief that death provides a passage into some kind
of nirvana, reunion, or happy other life. Fantasies such as these
are often preconscious or unconscious and may be difficult to
detect, although they may be powerful motives to self-destruction. Because of their comparatively hidden nature, they are
often overlooked. In the course of the mental state examination
one should try to determine what the patient imagines it would
be like to be dead.

Mistakes of Empathy and Intuition

At the present time it is impossible to predict future suicide
with any certainty through applying statistical principles to data
derived from existing patient profiles. Profiles assuredly will
identify persons at increased risk, but they are not helpful, once
a high risk group has been identified, in deciding which patients
will go on to take their lives and which will not. Discouraged
by this state of affairs, some students have publicly claimed that
clinical decisions about individual patients (once those at high
risk have been identified) must be made on the basis of "intuition."

This idea is not only incorrect; it is clinically dangerous,
because it encourages following hunches when careful formulation is in order. Psychodynamic formulation carries the clinician a step further than statistical analysis can. When a group
of patients has been identified at heightened risk, clinical examination can show the degree to which a given individual is
reliant on sustaining resources outside his own intrapsychic
structure, whether such resources are stably available, and

whether ego-regression is underway. There is a rational way to decide whether a patient is about to commit suicide after the usefulness of the patient "profile" has been exhausted, and it is not primarily intuitive.

Dangerous misjudgments can result from excessive reliance on clinical intuition. It is true that experienced clinicians sometimes develop a capacity to arrive at correct decisions about the comparative lethality of a given case without consciously working out a formulation, but the wise course is to examine intuitions carefully in the context of organized data in order to avoid bad decisions. Intuitions arise from preconscious and unconscious processes; the operation of wishes and attitudes beyond the examiner's awareness can distort judgment and lead to mistakes. Intuitions should be subjected to critical, thoughtful, conscious examination to see how they fit with what we know about the patient's reliance on sustaining resources and their availability to him at the moment of decision.

Empathy is the process by which one person can feel the inner experience of another person without being directly told about it. It is a vital tool in our work, both in clinical assessment and in treatment. In the course of professional development the capacity for empathy expands considerably; its workings occur in a mostly automatic way, preconsciously. But its correct clinical use demands a certain self-discipline. Empathy is not, after all, a mode of direct perception in itself, independent of ordinary communication. There is no special sense organ for empathy. Empathic impressions can be derived only by preconsciously organizing and sorting out ordinary sensory perceptions from the patient (Buie 1981). Many suicidal patients totally conceal their condition by providing no cues to it that will excite the observer's empathic sensitivity. Indeed, many of these patients behave in such a way so as to suggest continuing investment in life, interest in the future, and engagement with others. This they do in empathically convincing ways. Sometimes they do it with conscious intent; at other times the patient may be unconscious of the suicidal force at work within him. Indeed, suicidal impulses can be conscious, preconscious, or unconscious—so can the concealment of the impulses from a careful, empathic examiner.

There is special danger in relying on so-called "empathic assessment" to determine the suicidal risk where schizophrenic and borderline cases are involved. In the first place, the subjective experience of such individuals is often so far from that of the examiner that there is a generous margin wherein empathic mistakes may hatch. Most people have not experienced the profound sense of aloneness or the devastating shame of worthlessness that is the daily lot of very disturbed patients. Even when the therapist is very experienced and himself no stranger to such affects, it may be quite distressing for him to experience them even in an empathic way. The tendency is always there to ward them off by denial, isolation, or some other defense.

Furthermore, the mental state examination of some patients will not betray the clues necessary to evoke alarm in the empathic observer, which might enable him to recognize one of the subjective states that can accompany suicide. Fatal cases repeatedly come to attention in which patients were examined frequently by competent, able specialists, yet significant sectors of inner life pertaining to a deep and lethal suicide preoccupation remained concealed (in Case 13 the splitting of the body representation indicated by the robot illusion came to light only via a suicide note).

If the examiner's intuition tells him the patient is suicidal but there is no corroborating evidence for it (the patient may even disclaim it), the intuition may or may not be correct. One way to estimate intuition's validity is to search for perceived cues that the patient has unwittingly provided and the examiner has preconsciously registered. When the examiner can call the corroborating cues to mind, he may have good reason for trusting his empathic response. If, however, the patient claims not to be suicidal, is not psychotic, and empathically does not feel suicidal, no confidence can be placed in intuitive judgment. Suicide risk assessment should then rest strictly on the case formulation. Look in such instances to the state of the patient's sustaining resources.

Neglect of Sustaining Resources

Further errors can arise from failure to take into account the sources and reliability of emotional support, i.e., the patient's reliance on and the availability of sustaining resources. Very commonly a depressed or suicidal patient is admitted to the hospital and almost immediately improves in mental state. A patient who was overwhelmed with despair may soon appear cheerful, speak hopefully, and be discharged in a few days. Many such patients become dangerously depressed again following discharge from the hospital. Indeed, the situation is sometimes worse than it was before the first admission. The patient, having fallen ill again after what seemed to be a successful period of treatment, concludes he must be a failure. He does not come back for further care because he thinks he has disgraced himself by getting sick again or because he has decided he is beyond treatment.

Most relapses of this sort obviously result from the loss of the supportive hospital milieu; more precisely, they follow the loss of specific supportive individuals within the hospital network. Socially isolated patients who have no one may improve simply due to the warmth and care made available to them in a good psychiatric center. If their life circumstances outside the ward have not changed, however, hospital discharge simply deprives them of the emotional support that brought about the initial superficial improvement.

No suicidal individual can be discharged safely until case formulation shows what new supports have become available to the patient in the community outside the hospital that were not previously there, *and that he has engaged himself with them.* The horse led to water will not always drink. It is well to recall that many suicidal individuals are quite fastidious in selecting among the sustaining resources offered to them. Most but not all are willing enough to accept fresh relationships with other caring people. Some require instead a special sort of pet or interesting work of a certain description. Examining the patient's past history will provide the best guide.

Repeated experience in reviewing cases of preventable suicide has proven a vital principle: the mental status examination and empathic judgment are untrustworthy guides, especially if they suggest a patient is safe from suicide. The only reliable instrument of assessment is psychodynamic formulation. It is the only means through which the current sufficiency or insufficiency of sustaining resources for soothing and self-worth can be estimated.

The following case helped Buie and me grasp this principle, and the study of later suicide deaths has confirmed it.

Case 29. A middle-aged executive was highly successful in his work and family life. He was quiet, confidence-inspiring, and was often consulted about business and personal problems. His relationship with his wife was good; his four adolescent children were developing well. Though socially popular he preferred to spend his leisure time alone, designing and building architectural models. He appeared to be a hard-working, obsessional man whose personality was within the range of normal.

His early life had been difficult. His mother had suffered from tuberculosis before his birth; late in her pregnancy with him she relapsed, returned to a sanitorium, and there the patient was born. She remained in the sanitorium and the baby was taken away by his father to be cared for by a capable, loving paternal aunt. When he was a year and a half old, his mother came home. Very soon she became intolerant of her sister-in-law, who in response left the house. For the patient this experience seems to have been tantamount to changing mothers at a time when libidinal object constancy had not yet been achieved (Fraiberg 1969). His aunt was allowed little contact with him thereafter, although they established a relationship of some warmth late in his adolescence. He and his father, a laborer, were never close.

From late childhood the patient was a diligent worker; his school performance was outstanding. His peers liked him, but he shared few personal thoughts and feelings with them. He worked after school; there was no time for sports. He seems to have felt secure at home (his mother idolized him), and he was much gratified by the acclaim he received as a student and effective worker.

He supported himself through college, living at home and working half-time. Soon after the patient began college his father suffered a series of strokes, became bedridden, and for a full year lay dying in the next room, babbling and crying, to the distraction of his over-worked son. The mother was forced to go to work.

After the father died the young man's mother developed severe complications of diabetes. She grew progressively blind and a series of amputations almost immobilized her. Within two years she, too, began having strokes, and the patient, still working and going to school, determined not to see her suffer much further. He procured a poison which he planned to give her if she became more "gorked out." She died suddenly without his taking that step. As soon as he finished his schooling he moved across the country, vowing never to return to the city where he had suffered so much. For several years he carried the poison meant for his mother in his left pocket because it gave him a comfortable feeling; he did not feel so alone.

While he could to some degree care about other people, he could not allow himself fully to love. He married his wife because she expressed her love for him directly, asking no more than quiet affection in return. He was a solidly reliable husband and father, but she took the major responsibility for running the household and raising the children. He was especially invested in work and was quickly promoted upward. To each advancement at work he reacted with severe anxiety that would abate as he proved to himself that he could excel at the new level as he had before. The same anxious perfectionism had also been characteristic of him in school. Eventually he was transferred to a large city where he had no ties to become a branch manager for his corporation.

The promotion opened the door to even higher possibilities in his company. A month before the move the aunt who had cared for him in infancy died. Breaking his vow, he returned to the city where he had grown up, attended her funeral, and began to settle her affairs. In the new job the patient now became exceedingly anxious; his work performance suffered. Deprived of the gratification work success had provided him, his self-confidence faltered and a depression set in. The discovery that he was emotionally vulnerable struck a further blow at his tenuous self-esteem. The depression deepened, and hospitalization was finally required.

On admission the patient was in a state of severe psychomotor retardation. He felt deeply hopeless. There was no evidence of suicidal, nor of psychotic thinking. His wife was very supportive and competent. He was therefore placed on a partial hospitalization program, to spend nights and weekends at home. Antidepressant drugs were administered and psychotherapy was attempted. Months went by; improvement was very gradual. The patient resisted talking about himself in therapy and maintained a moderately friendly distance from everybody.

He was aware, as was the staff, that his disability insurance was almost exhausted. The corporation had filled his job position in the intervening months; what work he might resume with them once he recovered was uncertain. The patient's wife tried to be supportive but confided to the social worker that her love for him was getting exhausted. These circumstances moved the staff to consider administering electroconvulsive therapy despite the fact that the patient was clinically improved. He worried whether the treatment would make him "gork out." He was asked whether he was suicidal, and he convincingly denied it.

At this point the senior ward psychiatrist sought consultation with other colleagues. None examined the patient, but they were given the clinical information provided above. The consultants were unanimous in the opinion that the patient was seriously at risk for suicide and advised full-time hospital care.

The senior ward psychiatrist re-examined the patient in the light of this consultation. Although he felt his consultants reasoned plausibly, the crisis he faced had arisen before the psychodynamics of suicide had been systematically studied, and the importance of psychodynamic formulation fully appreciated. The consultants had not examined the patient as he had, and he was deeply impressed with his *empathic sense* that the patient was not suicidal. The examiner's intuitive understanding coincided with the patient's stated self-view, and it was clear that the patient's *mental status* had improved. Other members of the ward staff examined the patient. On the basis of empathic impressions, and in the absence of observable evidence of suicide readiness, they came to similar conclusions. The patient was judged not to be at risk for suicide and full-time hospital care was not arranged.

A few days later the patient became uncharacteristically loving with his family and oddly solicitous about his wife's difficulty getting to sleep. She worried about his sudden change but did not call the hospital as she had been asked to do in the event she developed any concerns. After she fell asleep the patient got out of bed, put his coveralls on over his pajamas, and drove his car to a gas station to fill up the tank. Then, proceeding to a cliff several miles away, he raced at great speed through the metal guard rails and over the side, plunging to the bottom. He died as the car smashed and burned. (Buie 1983)

In retrospect it was plain that this patient was a man without the necessary intrapsychic structure necessary to feel secure and hopeful in the face of stress. His past history demonstrated that apart from his wife other people were not useful to him as exterior sustaining resources. The tone of his life was darkened by the ungrieved losses of his aunt (he lost her twice—in infancy and again in adulthood), his father, and his mother. The past history further showed that he had been severely traumatized in the first years of life and that he had been for many years "wedded to his work." Indeed, the pattern of work perfectionism went well back into adolescence; it was difficulty in the most recent promotion that threw him into disequilibrium. Plainly, work was the patient's principal external sustaining resource.

Once he had planned homicide (euthanasia) for his mother. There was evidence of an active death-fantasy at a time of previous stress, when the patient felt that dying would relieve suffering and restore peace. He carried poison in his pocket.

This patient relied heavily on external sustaining resources— his wife and his work—for the holding, soothing, esteem, and confidence he needed to maintain self-equilibrium. Now he was beginning to lose his wife's caring, and he had lost his high level corporate position. Realistically, he was discouraged about his job future. He faced a financial crisis with the imminent loss of his disability pay.

By psychodynamic formulation one would expect severe anxiety, hopelessness, and despair. Yet the patient displayed none of these. One might expect violent rage at fate, against the fickle corporation, against the hospital staff for failing him. One might expect self-recrimination. None of these reactions was detectable in the mental state—no anger was visible.

If this patient is scored according to the risk estimator scale in the Appendix he emerges in the mid-range of moderate suicide risk. If one examines the history without formulating the patient's reliance on sustaining resources, noticing that these were failing him, one finds cause for some concern but not the gravest concern. He had lost both his parents, he was a white male in middle age, he was suffering from a major depression, there had been a recent bereavement. The mental state examination was reassuring. He did not "feel" suicidal to those responsible for his care.

Identification of traumatization in early childhood, the discovery of a homicidal plan in late adolescence, the hoarding of
poison, recognition of reliance on exterior sustaining resources,
appreciation that the failure of one (work) had precipitated the
present crisis, and that the other (wife) was weakening, all add
up to a major warning from the psychodynamic formulation.

Psychodynamic formulation illuminates this patient's life-long
tragic dependence on sustaining resources outside himself for
survival. Mental illness was precipitated through the loss of
such a resource, and the patient was thrown into a suicidal
crisis animated by the specific dynamic shifts discussed in Chapter 2.

This case demonstrates an error in the estimation of suicide
risk which is repeated over and over. Mental status examination
and empathic assessment suggest the lessening or the absence
of suicide potential. The patient seems clinically better, even
positively motivated to live. He denies any intention to commit
suicide. Then he is discharged, returned to work, or otherwise
deprived of the sustaining influence of the treatment situation.
The clinician prepared with a case formulation will appreciate
the significance of the patient's life circumstances that threaten
the loss of vital sustaining resources and the evolution of a
suicidal crisis. Without it, guided only by mental state observations and intuition, the unprepared clinician must expect to
be caught unawares and to lose patients to suicide.

Clinical assessment of suicide danger does not stop at the
initial consultation. As treatment proceeds, the formulation
needs to be applied repeatedly as decisions are made about the
patient's course and as his life circumstances shift.

Countertransference Mistakes

Errors arising from countertransference responses to suicidal
patients are more typically a problem once treatment is un-

derway, but they can occur in the first clinical encounter. The hate that suicidal patients arouse in those responsible for their care, particularly when the clinician is unaware of it, is very likely to distort clinical judgment. The two components of countertransference hate—malice and aversion—can interact in complex destructive ways unless the examiner is fully conscious of both and has them in good control (Maltsberger 1974). Malicious, sadistic impulses are harder for most of us to acknowledge and to entertain consciously than aversive ones are. One may take it for granted that patients who threaten suicide or self-mutilation will excite a certain degree of malice in most examiners. Many will feel quite uncomfortable when such impulses threaten to force through repression into conscious awareness. The consequent anxiety will make you want to get away from the patient—in a word, to respond aversively. Aversive action is a way to ward off increasing sadistic excitement; one wants to get away from the person who is provoking it.

Unfortunately, it is the aversive component of countertransference hate that is most likely to precipitate suicidal action. Suicidal patients have a much higher tolerance for sadomasochistic struggling than they have for deprivation of support systems. Operating under the sway of active but unconscious countertransference aversion, the examiner may rationalize getting rid of a patient before there has been an adequate opportunity to collect the necessary data and organize it into a psychodynamic formulation.

This may happen in busy emergency rooms. No doubt it goes far to explain how it is that patients, presenting themselves in distress, are referred from one diagnostic center to another. A veteran may be sent from the general hospital to the Veterans' Administration hospital to be evaluated, only to be told to come back to the outpatient clinic in the morning if he wishes to be seen. Patients without insurance will be sent off to the county hospital. Those who live in the wrong district will be referred to the correct district center without being seen. Shuttling despairing patients about in this way because of countertransference unwillingness to do an emergency evaluation can provoke suicide. Sometimes patients are so annoying to hospital staff members that the case formulation is ignored as an aversive rush is organized to justify premature discharge. Staff may collude to minimize the danger of sending a patient back into the community when he has proven tiring, irritating, and slow to improve.

Economic realities of the contemporary psychiatric department make it difficult to keep patients in the hospital for a long time. There may be substantial pressures on those responsible to abbreviate hospital stays. The staff, overtaxed by weeks or months of effort on behalf of an annoying but unresponsive patient, can easily overlook important aspects of the patient's history and life circumstances, labeling him manipulative, uncooperative, or otherwise unsuitable or unmeritorious for continued treatment investment. This is particularly likely to happen when the patient does not seem depressed or when he has not mentioned suicide for some time. The bland mental state examination can then be used to rationalize a discharge more motivated by hidden aversion than by a realistic evaluation of the patient's need for and access to sustaining resources.

Appendix A

The Examination of the Patient

The following outline for the examination of patients, typical of many others of its type, approximates the one currently in use in the psychiatric department of the Massachusetts General Hospital. A similar guide is distributed to every new psychiatric resident and to the medical students who rotate through our wards. Trainees in related disciplines such as psychology and social work have also welcomed it as a general guide and *aide memoire*. This version has been expanded somewhat to emphasize certain lines of inquiry necessary in evaluating and formulating suicide risk. I include it not with any illusion that it is particularly unique, but in the hope that it may prove useful to colleagues who, beginning their training, may welcome an outline to assist them in gathering information necessary for psychodynamic formulation.

The guide will apply to the evaluation of all psychiatric patients, of course, but items that are especially important where suicide is in question have been printed in italics for purposes of emphasis.

The Clinical History

The clinical history is the patient's biography, a selective arrangement of many details that records the patient's progress through life—his heredity, family, his development, his environment, the hurts and the blessings life has dealt him, his successes, failures, and his illness. What are his characteristic ways of dealing with others? How does he respond to stresses? On what is his self-esteem predicated? What factors and what combinations of events have contributed to his psychiatric collapse? What is the unique flavor of this individual? These are the matters to be inferred from the clinical history, called in psychiatry the **anamnesis,** i.e., a reminiscence.

The parts of the anamnesis are these:

I. *Informants.* Each of the informants' names, addresses, and telephone numbers should be included in the record. You may want to reach them later. Their relationship, attitude toward the patient, and reliability should be noted.

In no other medical specialty (except possibly neurology) is the history the patient gives more likely to be distorted and incomplete than in psychiatry. And in no other specialty is the anamnestic process so intimately related to the process of treatment. For this reason no anamnesis is complete without the unique perspective friends and family members can give.

II. *Identification of the patient.* We try to place the patient demographically by taking note of his age, sex, color, religion, marital state, work, and education.

III. *The chief complaint.* Record here a brief direct quotation from the patient explaining his ailment as he sees it.

IV. *The history of the present illness.* Specify as closely as you can when the patient's adaptation began to deteriorate and symptoms appeared. Note major and minor changes in thinking, mood, habits, personality, and relationships between the onset of difficulty and the time of admission. Can you identify a stress, loss, or other injury that seems to correspond closely in time to the development of the illness? Record it if you can as a possible precipitating stress. What important environmental changes or physical illnesses seem to play a role?

The history of the present illness should be detailed, coherent, and recorded in chronological order. It is the main focus of the first interview in clinical psychiatry, and is the place where we search for the significant shifts in the patient's life surroundings that may have overtaxed his adaptive capacities.

V. *Previous psychiatric history* is recorded after the present illness and should be described chronologically. What symptoms and problems have troubled the patient in the past? Where was he treated? When? What treatment did he receive? How did he feel about the care given? Describe *previous suicide attempts* with respect to method, intention, and social context.

VI. *The family history* records details about the patient's genetic and environmental beginnings and provides information for a perspective on the comparative riches, droughts, opportunities and deprivations he experienced as his personality developed against his family endowment. Describe any *suicides, suicide attempts,* or *suicide threatening* in the family.

A. *Genetic history.* It is important to record available details about mental illnesses in other family members as specifically as possible. If a relative has been psychotic, at what ages did illness first appear? Was it chronic, cyclical, or limited? Where and when did the illness occur? Are other family members prone to deviant behavior such as alcoholism, criminal activity, addiction? Are there eccentrics?

B. *Socio-cultural matrix of the family.* What is the racial, religious, social, and educational heritage of the patient? What has been the patient's reaction to it—did he attempt to repudiate it, modify it, or embrace it?

C. *Parents.* Describe the individual characters of the parents, their relationship with each other, and the nature and manner of dealing with family conflict. What were their standards, expectations, and ways of engaging or ignoring the patient? How was discipline handled? Is there a history of *child abuse, seduction, humiliation, rejection, cruelty?*

   In the event of divorce note the date of separation and the reactions of all parties. If a parent has died, when did it happen and how did the patient deal with the loss?

D. *Siblings.* The names, ages, and salient characteristics of each are recorded here, as well as the patient's attitudes toward the significant ones. Dates of miscarriages and deaths are recorded.

E. **Significant other family members and associates** may include grandparents, aunts, uncles, step-parents, close friends. Details about these should be included as part of the family background from which the rest of the patient's life history grows.

F. **Subjective reactions of family members to the patient** and his problems are an important part of the history and are best learned by first-hand interviewing. *Are important other people invested in the patient's survival? Does anyone seem indifferent or actively want the patient dead?*

VII. **The personal or developmental history** is a chronologically ordered account of the significant events, reactions, and experiences in the patient's life. Ideally it is presented not as an impersonal chronicle, but as an ordering of events that give some insight into a developing, growing person. While the presentation of selected, exact detail is necessary, the best clinical history is informed more by the spirit of a biographer than by that of a newspaper reporter or census taker.

Answers to all the following questions will not ordinarily find their way into the written record, but each of the following categories should be surveyed.

A. **Prenatal history.** Was the pregnancy wanted? Was the mother ill during pregnancy? Was the delivery easy or complicated? What was the mother's first reaction to seeing her new baby? How many previous pregnancies had the mother had?

B. **Infancy.** Date and place of birth. How was the infant fed? Was feeding difficult? Was the mother comfortable with her baby? *Could she comfort him?* What kind of temperament did the new baby show? Was he "good"? lively? colicky? Were motor and speech development normal? *Illnesses or surgery in first two years? Was the infant ever separated from the mother?* What reaction did the father display toward the new baby? Who was available to advise and support the parents? Were there *early separations?* *Foster home placement?* *Adoption?*

C. **Toddler phase.** What is known about motor and speech development? What temperament did the little child have— placid, aggressive, clinging, shy? What was the toilet training like and when was it finished? How long did the patient wet the bed? Was he a headbanger? Tantrum prone? How did he respond to new siblings? Were there illnesses, surgery, asthma, periodic vomiting, eating disturbances? *Unusual struggles for control over the patient's body?*

D. **Pre-school phase.** How did he speak, play, move about? How did he adapt to other children with whom he played at home, in the neighborhood, nursery school and kindergarten? Could he tolerate being away from his mother? Was he prone to soil or wet himself? Was he prone to nightmares? Was he phobic?

E. **Elementary school phase.** How did he manage the transition to first grade and subsequent grades? How did he take to his teachers and they to him? Did he progress normally? What were his academic skills and weaknesses? Was he absent from school very much? Describe his peers and his place in the group. Did he have friends? A special chum? Was he a bully or a scapegoat? Did he have favorite games and hobbies? Was the patient *accident-prone?* Excessively *perfectionistic?*

F. **Adolescence.** Was adolescence marked by any change in school performance? What clubs, activities, hobbies, interested him? Did the patient enjoy competitive games? crushes? dates? Who were the idealized figures? Date of menarche or first ejaculation? Religious attitudes? Was the patient prone to philosophical rumination? Fits of depression or even *despair?*

G. **Occupational history.** When did the patient begin work? Jobs held should be listed chronologically with wages, dates, reasons for changes. Relations with peers and employers should be asked about and noted down. *What responses has the patient shown to work stress or loss?*

H. **Military history.** When did the patient begin military service? Reasons for enlistment are noted if he volunteered. Record the branch of service, rank obtained, tasks performed, and where he served in chronological order. Was he decorated or disciplined? Where did he have combat experience and what kind was it? Were friends killed or injured? Is the patient guilty about his combat activity? Did he have a part in atrocities or "fragging"?

I. **Sexual history.** Earliest memories of childhood, sexual experiences may be elicited. What was the nature of his sexual education and what were the parent's attitudes toward sex? Perversions? Heterosexual and homosexual experiences? Promiscuity? Has the patient developed a capacity for tenderness in intercourse or is his style exploitative? *Does he seek out sexual contact to bolster self-esteem?*

J. **Marital history** involves enquiry about courtship, premarital intercourse, birth control, sexual compatibility, planning of pregnancies, attitudes toward pregnancies, children, conflicts about child rearing, problems, divorces, separations, and reactions to them. If a spouse has died, what happened and how did the patient respond? *Has the patient depended on the spouse to preserve self-esteem or emotional tranquility?*

K. **Medical history** is recorded as usual, but with special emphasis on the patient's reactions to illness and to their impact on his adaptation to work and personal living. Is there evidence of hypochondriasis or of a tendency to develop physical illness in response to stress?

VIII. **The premorbid personality.** As the history is elicited the examiner will accumulate enough general information to suggest to him an inchoate perspective on the patient's personality. Part of the artistry in preparing an anamnesis lies in following up selected hints and details from the mass at hand so that one obtains enough corroborative, illustrative particulars to write a vivid, original description of the premorbid character without cliché or vapid generalization. Give anecdotes. Quote directly. Capture the typical with a vignette. What can you record about the patient's social relationships, loves, work, failures, achievements, ambitions, dreams, standards, habits and mannerisms that will most palpably evoke his character for another reader? Is there a pattern of *alcohol* or other *substance abuse?* Is the patient prone to *suicidal daydreaming?* Is he prone to *panic when left alone, to fall into despair?* Is he *self-contemptuous?* Is he vulnerable to spells of *fury? How has he behaved when upset?*

The Mental State Examination

To examine systematically the patient's mental state and write down one's observations is to describe a mind in action at a discrete moment. If the anamnesis is a longitudinal survey of the patient's life, the mental state examination is an immediate specimen of the present. From this examination and the clinical history we derive diagnoses, empathic understanding, psychodynamic formulation, treatment plans, and prognoses. It is a major tool in psychiatry and is best mastered through disciplined, faithful practice. It is divided into seven parts: general appearance and behavior, stream of talk, mood, mental content, intellectual functioning, grasp, and judgment.

I. *General appearance and behavior.* Write down a description of the patient's bearing, mien, movements, and clothing in such a way that his image will appear in the reader's mind. Are there *scars* from previous self injuries? *Needle marks?*

   A. *Posture and bearing.* How does the patient stand or sit? How does he behave toward the examiner, the nurses? What does he do if placed in awkward positions? Are there tics, mannerisms, oddities? Is he mischievous, assaultive, withdrawn? Is he tense, languid, alert, or drowsy? Is there a tendency to imitate the position or movements of the examiner (echopraxia)?

B. **Facial expression.** What is the detailed appearance of the face and head? Does the patient look at the floor, at the examiner, or gaze into space? Does the patient tend to peer furtively out of the corners of his eyes? Is the chin downcast or haughtily raised? Is the mouth slack, compressed, pouting? Do the lips protrude? ("Schnauzkrampf")? If the patient smiles, what is its quality—vacant, silly, contemptuous? Do the eyes stare, blink, roll, droop, tear? Describe the brow. Is there blushing, perspiration, silent moving of the lips, licking, or other oddity of aspect? Does he look *tormented?* Is the patient clean-shaven? If not, describe the beard. How are cosmetics used? How is the hair worn? Does he seem to *listen to unseen others?*

C. **Motor activity.** Describe the patient's gait, muscle tone, and quality of movement. Does he slouch, pace, skip about, *wring his hands,* exhibit stereotypes, prolonged posturing? Is he *agitated?* Does he *pace?* Does he *strike himself?*

D. **Clothing.** The patient's choice of clothing and way of wearing it merits the most searching inspection. Take note of the style of the clothes and assess their appropriateness to the occasion, e.g., does the patient appear in the consulting room at 10:00 a.m. in a black décolleté gown and a pearl necklace? Is he fussily meticulous, flashy, grotesque in his choice of clothes? Are they inappropriately juvenile or old in cut? Are the colors bright or somber? What jewelry is there? Is the clothing clean or soiled, careless and untidy? Does he seem to have lost or gained weight?

E. **Other details.** Describe the condition of the patient's nails—clean? bitten? lacquered? Is there anything remarkable about the hands? Is the patient clean? Do you notice perfume or fetor?

II. **Stream of talk.** The form and quality of the patient's utterances are considered here, but not their content.

A. **Amplitude.** Does the patient whisper, shout, or vary the volume of his speech?

B. **Rate.** Is the speech rapid and tumbling, slow and hesitant?

C. **Quality.** Is the speech fluid, lively and spontaneous, merry, vivacious? Does the patient brook no interruption? Does he rhyme, pun, or sing? Is his speech choppy or incoherent? Scolding or abusive? Is it whining or clipped in tone? Anxiously urgent? Does the patient repeat stereotyped utterances? Perhaps the speech is halting, colorless and without inflection. Some patients drone, others are mute, and yet others seem to babble on pointlessly, moving from one subject to another, their direction influenced by casual sights and sounds. There may be peculiarities of speech, a penchant for high sounding, long or quaint words. Some patients may string together words and phrases that convey no intelligible meaning. In describing the stream of talk it is essential that the examiner record a sample of the talk he is studying, and that he avoid using such terms as "loose associations," "press of speech," "circumstantial speech" unless he first specifically documents what he means in writing. Far preferable to professional cant words are simple, clear descriptions in plain English, illustrated with a few examples.

III. **Mood.** Mood is the way the patient feels and refers to his state of emotion. For this reason the examiner asks him, "How are your spirits?" and tries to write down verbatim the most telling parts of his reply. To what the patient says about his mood may be added other observations that shed light on the question. To some extent mood assessment is guided by observations of the patient's general demeanor. One should try to notice whether the mood is appropriate to the mental content and to watch for lability. The patient may be sad, elated, fatuous, flat, ecstatic, lethargic, *despairing*. But a list of such adjectives is of no use in the clinical record unless the data which suggest them are written down.

Bear in mind that the superficially manifest affect may be quite at variance with the patient's inner mood. The patient may intentionally try to minimize any outward sign of his inner

despair for a variety of reasons. Compare your observations
with what the patient reports about his feelings.

Are there suicidal impulses? Does he want to attack anybody?
Does he feel he is dying? Does he feel irremediably alone? Does
he *hate himself?*

IV. **Mental content.** In this section take account of what the
patient is thinking, or any salient aspects of how he thinks it;
search specifically for disorders of perception and cognition.

   A. **Present concerns.** What are the preoccupations, worries,
wishes, demands that occupy the patient's mind at the
time of the examination? What is uppermost in his mind?
Try to notice exactly what he says in reply to the questions,
"What are you thinking?" and *"What hope have you for
the future?"*

   B. **Style of thinking.** Is the patient straightforward and
cooperative with the examiner, or suspicious and mis-
trustful? Does he blame other people and circumstances
for his predicament? Is he making particular use of one
or more of the major primitive defenses such as denial,
distortion of reality, projection? Do you find evidence of
the more mature defenses such as reaction formation,
displacement, turning against the self, intellectualization,
isolation, rationalization, repression, sublimation? If so, describe the data before labeling it.

      Look for disturbances in self-esteem in the patient's
spontaneous utterances—*evidences of self-devaluation,* or
grandiose self-inflation. Look also for his attitudes toward
others. *Does he have anyone he loves?* Is he haughty and
aloof, suspicious and contemptuous? Is he servile, syco-
phantic? Or does he seem to have an appropriate sense
of his own importance and that of others? *Does he value
his work? What about himself does he value?*

   C. **Disorders of perception.** Hallucinations are sensory
experiences for which no external stimuli exist. The term
derives from a Greek word **alyein** which means to wander
in mind. Hallucinations must be actively enquired after

and described with respect to content, quality, duration, place of occurrence, time of day, accompanying affect, and whether they take place when the patient is alone or together with others. Find out if they are preceded by an aura. Does the patient have *autoscopic experiences?*

1. **Auditory hallucinations.** In addition to the above general particulars, find out what is heard, how far away it seems, and from where the sound seems to come. If the patient hears a voice, ask him if it sounds like an animal, a man, a woman, several people, et cetera. *Does he hear voices commanding him to commit suicide?*

2. **Visual hallucinations** need to be described carefully with respect to organization, consistency, and content. Are they seen in colors?

3. **Gustatory hallucinations** often are related to delusions of being poisoned. What does the patient taste?

4. **Olfactory hallucinations** often accompany disorders of the uncus (temporal lobe).

5. **Tactile (haptic) hallucinations** involving odd sensations about the mouth, anus, and genitalia often mark the onset of paranoid schizophrenia. Some are experienced as the touch of a hand, the brush of lips; others seem unspeakably obscene and the patient may try to conceal them. Some patients hallucinate peculiar sensations of the skin, which they attribute to an infestation of unseen insects or worms (formication). Such phenomena suggest organic disorders.

6. **Visceral hallucinations** may involve all manner of pains, feelings of fullness, gnawings.

7. **Other pseudoperceptual experiences.** Does the patient experience himself as *physically empty, hollow, dead,* outside himself? *Does he feel he is unreal?* Does he have the experience of déjà vu?

8. **Pseudohallucinations,** usually visual, are hallucinations which the patient knows to be such in spite

of the vividness of the false percept. Hypnagogic phenomena are pseudohallucinations which take place as one drifts between sleep and waking. Oneiroid experiences include the pseudohallucinations that take place in states of pathologically narrowed consciousness, e.g., in intoxications, exhaustion, confusions.

9. *Perceptual illusions* differ from pseudohallucinations only in that pseudohallucinations occur without actual sensory stimulation, while illusions involve a transitory misinterpretation of some actual sensory experience. A perceptual illusion is a transient erroneous perception of a real sensory stimulus.

D. *Disorders of cognition.* The mental state examination calls for careful description of any disorders in the connectedness and rate of thought. We also describe here conceptual illusions, morbid attitudes, preoccupations, and delusions.

1. *Disorders in the connectedness of thoughts*

    a) Looseness of associations, one of the fundamental marks of schizophrenia, is difficult to define and is often confused with other phenomena such as press of speech (which refers to an urgency of utterance). Certainly it is characterized by a disconnectedness of thought and by the putting together of manifestly disconnected ideas. But it is more than that—the patient is vague; he illogically switches off onto seemingly unrelated side issues. Thought is directed by alliterations, analogies, symbolic meanings, clang associations, and condensations. Words are used concretely, quixotically. There is no discernible purpose in the flow of ideas. Because this term is so commonly misunderstood the examiner should always write down a verbatim specimen in the record, just as Eugen Bleuler did in presenting the following example of loose association:

"Olive-oil is an Arabian liquor-sauce which the Afgans, Moors and Moslems use in ostrich-farming. The Indian plantain-tree is the whiskey of the Parsees and Arabs. The Parsee or Caucasian possesses as much influence over his elephant as does the Moor over his dromedary. The camel is the sport of Jews and Arabs. Barley, rice, and sugar cane called artichoke, grow remarkably well in India. The Brahmins live as castes in Beluchistan. The Circassians occupy Manchuria in China. China is the Eldorado of the Pawnees."*

A grossly incoherent spate of loose associations is sometimes called a word salad. A clang association is an association based on similarity of sounds without regard for differences in meaning; it is found in the manic phase of manic depressive disorder as well as in schizophrenia.

b) **Blocking.** Blocking is an abrupt interruption of thinking in the middle of a train of ideas. If the patient is speaking he may halt in mid-sentence and sit mutely for a moment or longer, unable to explain what has happened. The patient may experience this phenomenon as something which happens to him without his having any control over it. Bleuler considered a positive response to the question, "Do you ever experience a deprivation of thoughts" as pathognomonic of a schizophrenic association disorder.

c) **Stereotypy** is the constant repetition of any action, including certain words or phrases.

d) **Echolalia** is the pathological repetitive imitation of the speech of another.

e) **Klebendenken** refers to adhesive, perseverative thinking in which certain ideas or phrases seem senselessly attached to each other.

* E. Bleuler, *Dementia Praecox or the Group of Schizophrenias* (New York: International Universities Press, 1980), 15.

    f) **Concretization** is the opposite of abstraction: specific detail is overemphasized; words do not represent differentiated, integrated concepts, but remain embedded in perceptual experience, relating very much to immediate sensation.

2. **Disorders of the rate of thinking.** Quite a separate matter from the rate of speech, the rate of thinking may vary markedly even when the patient is silent. Some patients complain that their thoughts race uncontrollably, while others are troubled by a very slow, intermittent flow of ideas. The patient will usually not tell you about this kind of trouble unless you ask about it.

3. **Conceptual illusions** are false beliefs based on ignorance or misinterpretation of facts, capable of correction by experience or evidence to the contrary. They may have great emotional value to the patient and are often surrendered reluctantly. An example of a conceptual illusion is the **idea of reference,** the impression that the smiles, talk, or activity of others have direct, usually malignant, reference to the patient himself when such is not so. Ideas of reference do not as such involve the element of lasting conviction.

4. **Morbid preoccupations**

    a) **Erroneous convictions and beliefs respecting personal worth** very often accompany affective disorders. Some patients are self-critical globally or about certain sectors of their lives. Others have inflated estimates of their capacities and importance to family, associates, or society at large.

    b) **Hypochondriacal concerns** may dominate the thinking of the patient.

    c) **Suicidal brooding** should be assessed in all patients who suffer from depressed mood and a serious effort made to assess to what degree such

thinking is accompanied by *impulses* to commit
suicide.

d) **Homicidal or violent brooding** should be
carefully assessed in a similar way.

e) **Compulsive phenomena.** In psychiatry a ritual
is a frequently repeated formula of thoughts, words,
or acts that the patient feels driven to perform
but that makes no manifest sense. Under this
rubric one looks for such problems as a hand-
washing compulsion, a compulsion to touch certain objects (délire de toucher), to think or repeat
certain words or sentences for magical purposes
(including certain kinds of praying).

f) **Obsessive phenomena.** Obsessive thoughts, the
intrusion of nonsensical or occasionally shocking
ideas into the midst of the stream of consciousness,
may trouble some patients, e.g., a deeply religious
person who cannot keep from thinking blas-
phemies during the most solemn moments of
worship. Others may suffer from obsessive preoccupations. Certain ideas, fears, causes, or projects
dominate their thinking. In monomania the patient can think of one subject only.

g) **Delusions.** A delusion is an unshakeably fixed
conviction of improbable content uncontrovertible
by experience or evidence to the contrary and
unsupported by the patient's subculture. An idea
of reference becomes a **delusion of persecution**
when the patient grows convinced that another
person or group is set against him to work him
some ill. Separate delusions of deserved persecution from delusions of unjust persecution. A
somatic delusion expresses a false belief about
the patient's own body. Some patients experience
violent emotional states in which they are sure
the world is ending, the earth is disintegrating,

that final chaos is at hand **(Weltuntergang Er-lebnis).** Some delusions may be closely related to the patient's disturbed self-esteem; one man may be so convinced of his profound wickedness that he forms the delusion that an executioner should be and is on the way to put him to death. Another, so inflated with a sense of power and importance, declares that he is the Messiah come at last **(delusion of grandeur).** Close study of the contents of individual delusions in the context of the clinical history will generally reveal the interplay of projection, distortion, lost reality testing, incapacity for self-object differentiation, symbolism, condensation, and intense wishes.

V. **Intellectual functions.** The patient's capacity to orient himself to the environment, to register new impressions, to retain and recall them, to concentrate, to apprehend and to form correct judgments, are systematically assessed.

  A. **Orientation**
    1. **To time.** Does the patient know the day of the week, the month, the day of the month, the year, the time of day?
    2. **To place.** Does he know where he is? The address? The name of the hospital? Where he is in it? The city? The state?
    3. **To persons.** Does he know who the people are about him, their names? Their purposes in being there?
    4. **To situation.** Does he understand why he is in the hospital?
    5. **To self.** Does he know who he is and what his relationship is to others around him?
  B. **Attention.** Does the patient pay attention? You may wish to read a series of words, digits or letters to the patient and ask him to raise his finger each time a specified one is repeated.

C. Memory.

1. **Remote.** Compare what the patient says about his life history with the accounts provided by others. Can the patient recall the place he was born? His mother's maiden name? The date of his marriage? Names of teachers? Names, ages, years of birth of children?

2. **Recent.** Does the patient know how he arrived at the hospital? When? With whom? Can he recall what he had for breakfast, what the headlines were in the morning newspaper?

D. Fund of information. How many presidents can the patient name correctly in retrograde order? Can he name ten colors, countries, vegetables, animals? How many states and countries can he name? Inventors, writers, famous athletes, politicians?

E. Retention and capacity for recall

1. **Digit retention.** Determine how many digits forward the patient can recall, and how many backward. Digits should be spoken to the patient in an even tone at about one second intervals.

2. **Test items.** Tell the patient that you want him to remember three items, and that you will ask him to repeat them in five minutes. Then mention an address, a book title, and a color, e.g., 345 Oxford Street, Cambridge; **Gone With the Wind;** Purple. Can the patient recall the examiner's name?

3. **Test stories** not only give some indication of capacity for retention and recall, but are often selectively distorted, forgotten, or elaborated in ways that suggest areas of emotional conflict. The examiner would do well to memorize one of the test stories below so that he will always have it available. The story is recited to the patient after explaining that he will be asked to repeat it as exactly as he can. The patient may be asked to explain the story after he has tried to repeat it.

The Story of the Gilded Boy

At the coronation of one of the Popes about 300 years ago a little boy was chosen to play the part of an angel. In order that his appearance might be as magnificent as possible, he was covered from head to foot with a coating of gold foil. The little boy fell ill, and although everything possible was done for his recovery except the removal of the fatal golden covering, he died within a few hours.

The Cowboy Story

A cowboy went to San Francisco with his dog, which he left at a friend's while he went to buy a new suit of clothes. Dressed in his brand new suit of clothes he came back to the dog, whistled to it, called it by name, and patted it. But the dog would have nothing to do with him in his new coat and hat, and gave a mournful howl. Coaxing was of no avail, so the cowboy went away and put on his old suit and the dog immediately showed its wild joy on seeing its master as it thought he ought to be.

F. Calculation. The patient is asked to subtract 7 from 100 and from each consecutive remainder. If the patient is practiced at this test, ask him to subtract serial 3's instead. Record the patient's answers and the time he requires to give them. Most people can perform this task in about a minute.

G. Capacity for abstraction. Some patients are limited in their capacity to generalize, tending to overemphasize specific detail and immediate experience. We describe such thinking as concrete. The patient's capacity to abstract may be tested by asking him to explain proverbs, e.g., "A rolling stone gathers no moss," "People who live in glass houses shouldn't throw stones," "Flies don't get into a shut mouth." The patient may also be asked to explain the similarities between such pairs as an apple and an orange, ice cream and pea soup, a lobster and an oak tree, honesty and laziness.

VI. *Grasp.* To what extent does the patient understand that he is ill? What is his attitude toward his condition and toward being in the hospital? Can he acknowledge problems, incapacities?

VII. *Judgment.* How appropriately does he cooperate in his treatment? Does he understand and behave appropriately with respect to his financial or other personal responsibilities?

Appendix B

Risk Estimator for Suicide

General Information

The Risk Estimator for Suicide is a scale designed to estimate the risk of suicide in adults aged 18–70 years during the 2-year period following the time of assessment.

This scale is primarily applicable to persons known to be at some risk, such as those in a serious depressive state, those who have suicidal thoughts or impulses, or those who have made a recent suicide attempt.

This scale is to be administered by a clinician, not self-administered. Responses to the items in the first column of the Risk Factor Scoring Table are best determined in the course of a clinical interview. The information need not be obtained in the listed order.

The subjective judgment of the interviewer is to be used throughout in categorizing each response, because data provided in the clinical situation may be incomplete, ambiguous, or conflicting.

The Risk Estimator for Suicide is intended as a supplement to, not a substitute for, clinical judgment. A thorough evaluation is indicated in any serious emotional disturbance. *Individual uniqueness suggests that when the scale is not consistent with clinical judgment, clinical judgment should be given precedence.*

Instructions

1. In the Age Scoring Table, circle the score that corresponds to the patient's age.

2. Identify the *one* most appropriate response category in the second column of the Risk Factor Scoring Table and circle the corresponding score. *If data are missing or unobtainable, leave the item unmarked.*

3. Total the circled scores and determine from the Table of Risk the indicated category of risk.

Age Scoring Table

Age	Score	Age	Score	Age	Score	Age	Score
18	0	32	36	46	65	60	90
19	3	33	39	47	67	61	91
20	6	34	41	48	69	62	93
21	9	35	43	49	71	63	95
22	12	36	45	50	72	64	96
23	14	37	47	51	74	65	98
24	17	38	49	52	76	66	99
25	20	39	51	53	78	67	101
26	22	40	53	54	80	68	102
27	25	41	55	55	81	69	104
28	27	42	57	56	83	70	106
29	29	43	59	57	85		
30	32	44	61	58	86		
31	34	45	63	59	88		

Risk Factor Scoring Table

Item	Response Category	Score
1. Age at last birthday	See Age Scoring Table	—
2. Type of occupation	Executive, administrator, or professional	48
	Owner of business	48
	Semiskilled worker	48
	Other	0
3. Sexual orientation	Bisexual, sexually active	65
	Homosexual, not sexually active	65
	Other	0
4. Financial resources	None or negative (debts exceed resources)	0
	0 to $100	35
	More than $100	70
5. Threat of significant financial loss	Yes	63
	No	0
6. Special stress: unique to subject's circumstances, *other than* loss of finances or relationship, threat of prosecution, illegitimate pregnancy, substance abuse, or poor health.	Severe	63
	Other	0
7. Hours of sleep per night (approximate nearest whole hour)	0–2	0
	3–5	37
	6 or more	74
8. Change or weight during present episode of stress (approximate)	Weight gain	60
	Less than 10% weight loss	60
	Other	0
9. Ideas of persecution or reference	Moderate or severe	45
	Other	0
10. Intensity of present suicidal impulses	Questionable, moderate, or severe	100
	Other	0
11. If current suicide attempt made, seriousness of intent to die	Unequivocal	88
	Ambivalent, weighted toward suicide	88
	Other or not applicable	0

Risk Factor Scoring Table (continued)

Item	Response Category	Score
12. Number of previous psychiatric hospitalizations	None	0
	1	21
	2	43
	3 or more	64
13. Results of previous efforts to obtain help	No previous efforts	0
	Some degree of help	0
	Poor, unsatisfactory, or variable	55
14. Emotional disorder in family history	Depression	45
	Alcoholism	45
	Other	0
15. Interviewer's reaction to the person	Highly positive	0
	Moderately or slightly positive	42
	Neutral or negative	85
Total score		—

Table of Risk

Total Score	Decile of Risk	Relative Risk	Approximate 2-Year Suicide Rate
0–271	1	Very low	Less than 1%
272–311	2	Low	1.0%–2.5%
312–344	3	Low	1.0%–2.5%
345–377	4	Moderate	2.5%–5.0%
378–407	5	Moderate	2.5%–5.0%
408–435	6	Moderate	2.5%–5.0%
436–465	7	Moderate	2.5%–5.0%
466–502	8	High	5.0%–10.0%
503–553	9	High	5.0%–10.0%
554 and over	10	Very high	More than 10.0%

Bibliography

Abraham, K. "A Short Study of the Development of the Libido, Viewed in the Light of Mental Disorders." (1924) In *The Selected Papers of Karl Abraham, M.D.*, B. Douglas and A. Strachey. New York: Basic Books, 1953.

Adler, G., and D. H. Buie. "Aloneness and Borderline Psychopathology: The Possible Relevance of Child Developmental Issues." *Int. J. Psychoanal.* (1979) 60:83-96.

Alvarez, A. *The Savage God, A Study of Suicide.* New York: Random House, 1972.

Andersen, H. C. "The Snow Queen." In *Fairy Tales and Legends by Hans Andersen*, London: The Bodley Head, 118-151, 1935.

Arlow, J. "Notes on Oral Symbolism" *Psychoanal. Quart.* (1955) 24:63-74.

Asberg, M., and others. "5-HIAA in the Cerebrospinal Fluid. A Biochemical Suicide Predictor." *Arch. Gen. Psychiat.* (1976) 33:1193-1197.

Baechler J. *Suicides.* B. Cooper, New York: Basic Books, 1975.

Barraclough, B., and others. "A Hundred Cases of Suicide: Clinical Aspects." *Brit. J. Psychiat.*, (1974) 125:355-373.

Beck, A. T., and others. "The Measurement of Pessimism: The Hopelessness Scale." *J. Consult. and Clin. Psychol.* (1974) 42:861-865.

Beck, A. T., and others. "Hopelessness and Suicidal Behavior, an Overview." *J. Amer. Med. Assn.*, (1975) 234:1146-1149.

Beck, A. T., and others. "Classification of Suicidal Behaviors: I. Quantifying Intent and Medical Lethality," *Amer. J. Psychiat.*, 132:285-287, 1975.

Bibring, E. "The Mechanism of Depression." In P. Greenacre, ed. *Affective Disorders.* New York: International Universities Press: 1953, 13-48.

Birtchnell, J. "The Relationship between Attempted Suicide, Depression and Parent Death." *Brit. J. Psychiat.* (1970) 116:307-313.

Bleuler, E. *Textbook of Psychiatry*. A. A. Brill, trans. New York: Macmillan, 1924.

Brown, G. L., and others. "Aggression, Suicide, and Serotonin: Relationships of CSF Amine Metabolites." *Amer. J. Psychiat.* (1982) 139:741–746.

Buie, D. H. "Empathy: Its Nature and Limitations." *J. Amer. Psychoanal. Assn.* (1981) 29:281–307.

Buie, D. H., and G. Adler. "Definitive Treatment of the Borderline Patient." *Int. J. Psychoanal. Psychother.* (1982) 9:51–87.

Buie, D. H., and John T. Maltsberger. "The Practical Formulation of Suicide Risk." Cambridge, Massachusetts: The Firefly Press, 1983.

Carroll, J., and others. "Family Experiences of Self-Mutilating Patients." *Amer. J. Psychiat.* (1980) 137:852–853.

Corey, D., and V. R. Andress. "Alcohol Consumption and Suicidal Behavior." *Psychol. Reports* (1977) 40:506.

Dabrowski, C. "Psychological Bases of Self-Mutilation." *Psychol. Monographs* (1937) 19:1–104.

Davis, R. "Black Suicide in the Seventies: Current Trends." *Suicide and Life Threat. Behav.* (1979) 9:131–140.

Dorpat, T. L., and H. S. Ripley. "A Study of Suicide in the Seattle Area." *Comp. Psychiat.* (1960) 1:349–359.

Dorpat, T. L., and J. W. Boswell. "An Evaluation of Suicidal Intent in Suicide Attempts." *Comp. Psychiat.* (1963) 4:117–125.

Dorpat, T. L., and others. "Broken Homes and Attempted and Completed Suicide." *Arch. Gen. Psychiat.* (1965) 12:213–216.

Dorpat, T. L., and others. "The Relationship between Attempted Suicide and Committed Suicide." *Comp. Psychiat.* (1967) 8:74–79.

Dorpat, T. L., W. F. Anderson, and H. S. Ripley. "The Relationship of Physical Illness to Suicide." H. L. P. Resnik, ed. *Suicidal Behaviors*. Boston: Little Brown and Co., 1968, 209–219.

Dorpat, T. L. "Drug Automatism, Barbiturate Poisoning, and Suicide Behavior." *Arch. Gen. Psychiat.* (1974) 31:216–220.

Drake, R. E., and others. "Suicide Among Schizophrenics: Who is at Risk?" *J. Nerv. Ment. Dis.* (1984) 172:613–617.

Ettlinger, R. W. "Suicides in a Group of Patients Who Had Previously Attempted Suicide." *Acta Psychiat. Scand.* (1964) 40:363–378.

Emery, G. D., and others. "Depression, Hopelessness, and Suicidal Intent Among Heroin Addicts." *Int. J. Addict.* (1981) 16:425–429.

Exner, J. E., and J. Wylie. "Some Rorschach Data Concerning Suicide." *J. Pers. Assess.* (1977) 41:339–348.

Farberow, N. L., E. S. Shneidman, and C. Neuringer. "Case History and Neuropsychiatric Hospitalization Factors in Suicide." (1961) E. S. Shneidman et al. ed. *The Psychology of Suicide*. New York: Science House, 1970, 385–402.

Fedden, H. R. *Suicide, A Social and Historical Study.* London: Peter Davies, 1938.

Fraiberg, S. "Libidinal Object Constancy and Mental Representation." *Psychoanal. Study of the Child* (1969) 24:9–47.

Frederick, C. J. "Suicide in Young Minority Group Persons." H. S. Sudak and others, ed. *Suicide in the Young.* Boston: John Wright/PSG: 1984, 31–44.

Freud, S. *The Interpretation of Dreams.* In *Standard Edition* 4 (1900). London: Hogarth Press, 1961.

Freud, S. "On Narcissism: An Introduction." In *Standard Edition* 14 (1914). London: Hogarth Press, 1957, 67–102.

Freud, S. "Mourning and Melancholia." In *Standard Edition* 14 (1917). London: Hogarth Press, 1957, 237–258.

Freud, S. "The Uncanny." In *Standard Edition* 17 (1919). London: Hogarth Press, 1961, 217–256.

Freud, S. "The Ego and the Id." In *Standard Edition* 19 (1923). London: Hogarth Press, 1961, 3–66.

Freud, S. "Inhibitions, Symptoms, and Anxiety." In *Standard Edition* 20 (1926). London: Hogarth Press, 1957, 77–178.

Freud, S. "An Outline of Psychoanalysis." In *Standard Edition* 23 (1938). London: Hogarth Press, 1957, 141–207.

Furman, E. "Some Difficulties in Assessing Depression and Suicide in Childhood." In H. S. Sudak and others, ed. *Suicide in the Young.* Boston: John Wright/PSG:1984, 245–258.

Furst, S. S., and M. O. Ostow. "The Psychodynamics of Suicide." In L. D. Hankoff, ed. *Suicide, Theory and Clinical Aspects.* Littleton, Massachusetts: PSG:1979, 165–178.

Glover, E. "Grades of Ego Differentiation." (1930) In *On the Early Development of the Mind.* London: Imago: 1956, 112–122.

Goethe, J. *The Sorrows of Young Werther.* (1774) Catherine Hutter, trans. New York: New American Library, 1962.

Goldney, R. D. "Parental Loss and Reported Childhood Stress in Young Women Who Attempt Suicide." *Acta Psychiat. Scand.* (1981) 64:34–47.

Green, A. H. "Self-Destructive Behavior in Battered Children." *Amer. J. Psychiat.* (1978) 135:579–582.

Hartmann, H. *Ego Psychology and the Problem of Adaptation.* D. Rapaport, trans. New York: International Universities Press, 1939.

Havens, L. "The Placement and Movement of Hallucinations in Space: Phenomenology and Theory." *Int. J. Psychoanal.* (1962) 43:426–435.

Hendin, H. "Psychotherapy and Suicide." *Amer. J. Psychother.* (1981) 35:469–480.

Hendrick, I. "Suicide as Wish Fulfilment." *Psychiat. Quart.* (1940) 14:30–42.

Henseler, H. "The Suicidal Act from the Standpoint of the Psychoanalytic Theory of Narcissism." *Psyche* (1975) 29:191–207.

Hilgard, J. R. "Depressive and Psychotic States as Anniversaries to Sibling Death in Childhood." *Int. Psychiat. Clinics* (1969) 6:197–211.

Holinger, P. C., and D. Offer. "Toward the Prediction of Violent Deaths Among the Young." In Sudak, H. S. and others, ed. *Suicide in the Young.* Boston: John Wright/PSG: 1984, 15–29.

Jacobson, E. *The Self and the Object World.* New York: International Universities Press, 1964.

Jenson, V. W., and T. Petty. "The Fantasy of Being Rescued in Suicide." *Psychoanal. Quart.* (1958) 27:327.

Jones, E. "On 'Dying Together', with Special Reference to Heinrich von Kleist's Suicide." (1911) *Essays in Applied Psycho-Analysis*, vol. 1. London: Hogarth Press, 1951, 9–15.

Kanzer, M. "Writers and the Early Loss of Parents." *J. Hillside Hospital* (1953) 2:148–151.

Keeler, M. H., and C. B. Reifler. "Suicide During an L.S.D. Reaction." *Amer. J. Psychiat.* (1967) 123:884–885.

Kendall, R. E. "Alcohol and Suicide." *Subst. Alcohol Actions Misuse* (1983) 4:121–127.

Kernberg, O. "A Psychoanalytic Classification of Character Pathology." *J. Amer. Psychoanal. Assn.* (1970) 18:800–822.

Klein, M. *Envy and Gratitude and Other Works.* New York: Delacorte Press, 1975.

Kohut, H. *The Analysis of the Self: A Systematic Approach to the Psychoanalytic Treatment of Narcissistic Personality Disorders.* New York: International Universities Press, 1971.

Koranyi, E. K. "Fatalities in 2,070 Psychiatric Outpatients." *Arch. Gen. Psychiat.* (1977) 34:1137–1142.

Kovacs, M., and others. "Hopelessness: An Indicator of Suicidal Risk," *Suicide* (1975) 5:90–103.

Kraepelin, E. "Introduction: Melancholia." In T. Johnston, trans. *Lectures on Clinical Psychiatry.* New York: Hafner Publishing Co., 1968, 1–10. (This is a reprint of the original 1904 edition, published in London by Bailliere, Tindall and Cox.)

Lester, D., and A. Beck. "Early Loss as Possible 'Sensitizer' to Later Loss in Attempted Suicides." *Psychol. Reports* (1976) 39:121–122.

Lester, D., and others. "Extrapolation from Attempted Suicides to Completed Suicides: A Test." *J. Abnormal Psychol.* (1979) 88:78–80.

Levi, L. D., and others. "Separation and Attempted Suicide." *Arch. Gen. Psychiat.* (1966) 15:158–164.

Lidberg, L., and others. "5-Hydroxyindoleacetic Acid Levels in Attempted Suicides Who Have Killed Their Children." [a letter to the editor] *Lancet* (October 20, 1984) 928.

Linden, L. L., and W. Breed. "The Demographic Epidemiology of Suicide." In E. S. Shneidman, ed. *Suicidology: Contemporary Developments*. New York: Grune and Stratton, 1976, 71–98.

Lishman, W. *Organic Psychiatry*. Oxford: Blackwell Scientific, 1978.

Litman, R. E., and C. Swearingen. "Bondage and Suicide." *Arch. Gen. Psychiat.* (1972) 27:80–85.

Lukianowicz, N. "Autoscopic Phenomena." *Arch. Neurol. and Psychiat.* (1958) 80:199.

Mahler, M., and others. *The Psychological Birth of the Human Infant*. New York: Basic Books, 1975.

Maltsberger, J. T., and D. H. Buie. "Countertransference Hate in the Treatment of Suicidal Patients," *Arch. Gen. Psychiat.* (1974) 30:625–633.

Maltsberger, J. T., and D. H. Buie. "The Devices of Suicide, Revenge, Riddance, and Rebirth." *Int. Rev. Psychoanal.* (1980) 7:61–72.

Maltsberger, J. T. "Consultation in a Suicidal Impasse." *Int. J. Psychoanal. Psychother.* (1984) 10:131–171.

Margolin, N. L., and J. D. Teichet. "Thirteen Adolescent Male Suicide Attempts, Dynamic Considerations." *J. Amer. Acad. Child Psychiat.* (1968) 7:296–315.

Marshall, J. R., and others. "On Precipitating Factors: Cancer as a Cause of Suicide." *Suicide and Life Threat. Behav.* (1983) 13:15–27.

Maugham, S. *Of Human Bondage*. New York: Sundial Press, 1915.

Menninger, K. A. "Psychoanalytic Aspects of Suicide." *Int. J. Psychoanal.* (1933) 14:376–390.

Menninger, K. *Man Against Himself*. New York: Harcourt, Brace & World, 1938.

McEvoy, T. L. "A Comparison of Suicidal and Non-Suicidal Patients by Means of the Thematic Apperception Test." *Dissert. Abstracts* (1963) 24:1248.

Meyerson, L. R., and others. "Human Brain Receptor Alterations in Suicide Victims." *Pharmacol. Biochem. Behav.* (1982) 17:159–163.

Miles, Charles P. "Conditions Predisposing to Suicide, a Review." *J. Nerv. Ment. Dis.* (1977) 164:231–246.

Minkoff, K., and others. "Hopelessness, Depression, and Attempted Suicide." *Amer. J. Psychiat.* (1973) 130:455–459.

Moss, L. M., and D. M. Hamilton. "the Psychotherapy of the Suicidal Patient." *Amer. J. Psychiat.* (1956) 112:814–820.

Motto, J. A. "The Psychopathology of Suicide: A Clinical Model Approach." *Amer. J. Psychiat.* (1979) 136:516–520.

Motto, J. A., and others. "Development of a Clinical Instrument to Estimate Suicide Risk." *Amer. J. Psychiat.* (1985) 142:680–686.

Murphy, G. E., and E. Robins. "Social Factors in Suicide." *J. Amer. Med. Assn.* (1967) 199:303–308.

Murphy, G. E., and E. Robins. "The Communication of Suicidal Ideas." In H. L. P. Resnik, ed. *Suicidal Behaviors.* Boston: Little Brown, 1968, pp. 163–170.

Murphy, G. E., J. W. Armstrong, Jr., S. L. Hermele, and others. "Suicide and Alcoholism: Interpersonal Loss Confirmed as a Predictor." *Arch. Gen. Psychiat.* (1979) 36:65–69.

Murphy, G. E., and R. D. Wetzel. "Family History of Suicidal Behavior Among Suicide Attempters." *J. Nerv. Ment. Dis.* (1982) 170:86–90.

Murphy, G. E. "The Prediction of Suicide—Why is it so Difficult?" *Amer. J. Psychother.* (1985) 38:341–349.

Neuringer, C. "Suicide and the Rorschach: A Rueful Postscript." *J. Personal. Assessment* (1974) 38:535–539.

Niskanen, P., and others. "Suicides in Helsinki Psychiatric Hospitals in 1964–1972." *Psychiatria Fennica* (1974):275–280.

Novick, J. "Attempted Suicide in Adolescence: The Suicide Sequence." In H. S. Sudak and others, ed. *Suicide in the Young.* Boston: John Wright/PSG, 1984, 115–137.

Novotny, P. "Self-Cutting." *Bull. Menninger Clinic* (1972) 36:505–514.

Ostow, M. "The Metapsychology of Autoscopic Phenomena." *Int. J. Psychoanal.* (1960) 41:619–625.

Paerregaard, G. "Suicide among Attempted Suicides: a 10-year Follow-up." *Suicide* (1975) 5:140–144.

Petzel, S. V., and W. Cline. "Adolescent Suicide: Epidemiological and Biological Aspects." In S. Feinstein, ed. *Adolescent Psychiatry.* Chicago: University of Chicago Press, 1978.

Pfeffer, C. R. "Suicidal Behavior of Children: A Review with Implications for Research and Practice," *Amer. J. Psychiat.* (1981) 138:154–159.

Pfeffer, C. R. "Parental Suicide: An Organizing Event in the Development of Latency Age Children." *Suicide and Life Threat. Behav.* (1981) 11:43–50.

Piotrowski, Z. A. "Psychological Test Prediction of Suicide." In H. L. P. Resnik, ed. *Suicidal Behaviors.* Boston: Little Brown, 1968, 198–208.

Plath, S. *Ariel.* New York: Harper and Row, 1961.

Poe, E. A. "William Wilson." (1839) In P. F. Quinn, ed. *Edgar Allan Poe, Poetry and Tales.* New York: Library of America, 1984, 337–357.

Pollock, G. H. "Anniversary Reactions, Trauma, and Mourning." *Psychoanal. Quart.* (1970) 39:347–371.

Rainer, J. D. "Genetic Factors in Depression and Suicide." *Amer. J. Psychother.* (1985) 38:329–340.

Resnik, H. L. P. "Erotized Repetitive Hangings: A Form of Self-Destructive Behavior." *Amer. J. Psychother.* (1972) 26:4–21.

Robins, E., G. E. Murphy, R. H. Wilkonson, Jr., and others. "Some Clinical Considerations in the Prevention of Suicide Based on a Study of 134 Successful Suicides." *Amer. J. Public Health.* (1959) 49:888–899.

Robins, E. *The Final Months.* New York: Oxford University Press, 1981.

Roose, S. P., and others. "Depression, Delusions, and Suicide." *Amer. J. Psychiat.* (1983) 140:1159–1162.

Roy, A. "Self Mutilation." *Brit. J. Med. Psychol.* (1978) 51:201–203.

Roy, A. "Suicide in Chronic Schizophrenia." *Brit. J. Psychiat.* (1982) 141:171–177.

Roy, A. "Risk Factors for Suicide in Psychiatric Patients." *Arch. Gen. Psychiat.* (1982) 39:1089–1095.

Roy, A. "Family History of Suicide." *Arch. Gen. Psychiat.* (1983) 40:971–974.

Rydin, E., and others. "Rorschach Ratings in Depressed and Suicidal Patients with Low Levels of 5-Hydroxyindoleacetic Acid in Cerebrospinal Fluid." *Psychiatry Res.* (1982) 7:229–243.

Sabbath, J. C. "The Suicidal Adolescent—the Expendable Child." *J. Amer. Acad. Child Psychiat.* (1969) 8:272–289.

Salama, A., and D. M. Sizemore. "Observations on Suicide among Hospitalized Schizophrenics." *Hosp. Commun. Psychiat.* (1982) 33:940–941.

Sandler, J. "On the Concept of the Superego." *Psychoanal. Study of the Child* (1960) 15:128–162.

Sandler, J., and B. Rosenblatt. "The Concept of the Representational World." *Psychoanal. Study of the Child* (1962) 17:128–145.

Schafer, R. "The Loving and Beloved Superego in Freud's Structural Theory." *Psychoanal. Study of the Child* (1960) 15:163–188.

Schilder, P. *The Image and Appearance of the Human Body.* New York: International Universities Press, 1950.

Schuttler, R., and two others. "The Risk of Suicide in Schizophrenic Illness." *Psychiatria Clinica* (1976) 97–105.

Seneca, *Ad Lucillium Epistolae Morales.* R. M. Gummere, translator. London: William Heinemann, 1934. Epistles 58 and 70.

Shneidman, E. S., and N. L. Farberow. "Statistical Comparisons between Attempted and Committed Suicides." In N. L. Farberow and E. S. Shneidman, eds. *The Cry for Help.* New York: McGraw-Hill, 1961, 19–47.

Tabachnick, N. D., and N. L. Farberow. "The Assessment of Self-Destructive Potentiality." In N. L. Farberow and E. S. Shneidman, ed. *The Cry for Help.* New York: McGraw-Hill, 1961, 60–78.

Tolpin, M. "On the Beginnings of a Cohesive Self: An Application of the Concept of Transmuting Internalization to the Study of the Transitional Object and Signal Anxiety." *Psychoanal. Study of the Child* (1971) 26:316–354.

Traskman, L., and others. "Monoamine Metabolites in CSF and Suicidal Behavior." *Arch. Gen. Psychiat.* (1981) 38:631–636.

Tsuang, M. T. "Genetic Factors in Suicide." *Dis. Nerv. System* (1977) 38:498–501.

Virkkunen, M. "Attitude to Psychiatric Treatment Before Suicide in Schizophrenia and Paranoid Psychoses." *Brit. J. Psychiat.* (1976) 128:47–49.

Wetzel, R. D., and others. "Hopelessness, Depression, and Suicide Intent." *Arch. Gen. Psychiat.* (1976) 33:1069–1073.

Whitehorn, J. C. "Guide to Interviewing and Clinical Personality Study." *Arch. Neurol. and Psychiat.* (1944) 52:197–216.

Williams, T. *A Streetcar Named Desire.* New York: New Directions, 1947.

Winnicott, D. W. "The Capacity to be Alone." (1958) In *The Maturational Process and the Facilitating Environment.* New York: International Universities Press, 1965, 29–36.

Winnicott, D. W. "Transitional Objects and Transitional Phenomena." (1953) In *Through Paediatrics to Psycho-Analysis.* New York: Basic Books, 1975, 229–242.

Winokur, G., and M. Tsuang. "The Iowa 500: Suicide in Mania, Depression, and Schizophrenia." *Amer. J. Psychiat.* (1975) 132:650–651.

Yarden, P. E. "Suicide in Chronic Schizophrenia." *Brit. J. Psychiat.* (1982) 141:171–177.

Zilboorg, G. "Differential Diagnostic Types of Suicide." *Arch. Neurol. Psychiat.* (1936) 35:270–291.

Zilboorg, G. "Some Aspects of Suicide." *Suicide.* (1975) 5:131–139. [posthumously published address given at St. Elizabeth's Hospital, Washington, D. C., on 27 August 1938]

Index